D1409171

IDITAROD SPIRIT™

BY KIM HEACOX

FOREWORD BY JOE REDINGTON, SR.

DRAWINGS BY DONNA GATES-KING

GRAPHIC ARTS CENTER PUBLISHING COMPANY, PORTLAND, OREGON

To Dr. Tom Cooley, veterinarian and musher,
and to everyone who treats their dogs
with kindness and respect.

The photographs in IDITAROD SPIRIT appear in no chronological
or geographical order. They document the Iditarod Trail Sled Dog
Race, and other races as well, plus dogsledding for recreation and
as a way of life.

CONTENTS

International Standard Book Number 1-55868-067-5
Library of Congress Number 91-71223
© MCMXCI by Graphic Arts Center Publishing Company
P.O. Box 10306 • Portland, Oregon 97210 • 503/226-2402
All rights reserved.
No part of this book can be reproduced by any means
without written permission of the publisher.
Drawings © MCMXCI Donna Gates-King
Lyrics from the "Iditarod Trail Song"
© MCMLXXXIV Jim Varsos and Hobo Jim Music Co. ASCAP
Used by permission.
President • Charles M. Hopkins
Editor-in-Chief • Douglas A. Pfeiffer
Managing Editor • Jean Andrews
Designer • Robert Reynolds
Cartographer • Manoa Mapworks, Inc.
Color Separations • Wy'east Color, Inc.
Typographer • Harrison Typesetting
Printer • Dynagraphics, Inc.
Bindery • Lincoln & Allen
Printed and bound in the United States of America

◄ ◄ ◄ ◄ A dog team at twenty mph at the Campbell Airstrip in Anchorage.
◄ ◄ ◄ Rainy Pass and the Alaska Range behind him, Mark Nordman leaves
Rohn on the Iditarod Trail Sled Dog Race. ◄ ◄ Mike Madden near Paxson,
on the Copper Basin 300 Sled Dog Race. ◄ With his lead dog, Rex, charging
into a -30°F wind chill, Jeff Weintraub crosses 3,160-foot Rainy Pass, the highest
point on the Iditarod. ► Sled dogs Nitro and Sagan in Denali National Park.

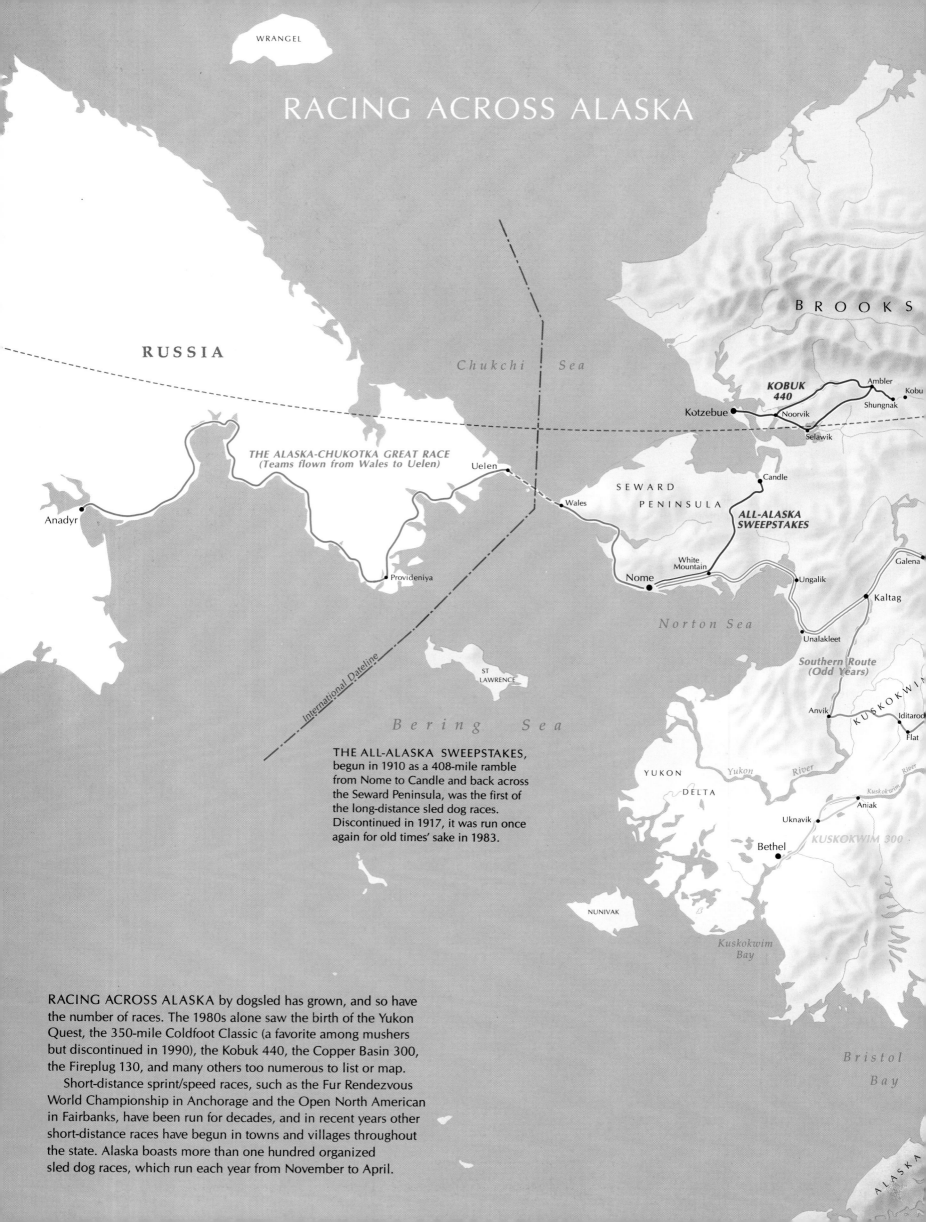

RACING ACROSS ALASKA

WRANGEL

BROOKS

RUSSIA

Chukchi Sea

KOBUK 440

Ambler

Kobu

Kotzebue   Noorvik   Shungnak

THE ALASKA-CHUKOTKA GREAT RACE
(Teams flown from Wales to Uelen)

Uelen

Selawik

SEWARD
PENINSULA

Candle

ALL-ALASKA
SWEEPSTAKES

Wales

Anadyr

White
Mountain

Galena

Providuniya

Nome

Ungalik

Kaltag

Norton Sea

Unalakleet

*Southern Route
(Odd Years)*

ST
LAWRENCE

KUSKOKWIM

Anvik

Iditarod

Bering   Sea

Flat

THE ALL-ALASKA SWEEPSTAKES,
begun in 1910 as a 408-mile ramble
from Nome to Candle and back across
the Seward Peninsula, was the first of
the long-distance sled dog races.
Discontinued in 1917, it was run once
again for old times' sake in 1983.

YUKON
DELTA

Yukon   River

*Kuskokwim
River*

Aniak

Uknavik

KUSKOKWIM 300

Bethel

NUNIVAK

*Kuskokwim
Bay*

RACING ACROSS ALASKA by dogsled has grown, and so have
the number of races. The 1980s alone saw the birth of the Yukon
Quest, the 350-mile Coldfoot Classic (a favorite among mushers
but discontinued in 1990), the Kobuk 440, the Copper Basin 300,
the Fireplug 130, and many others too numerous to list or map.
    Short-distance sprint/speed races, such as the Fur Rendezvous
World Championship in Anchorage and the Open North American
in Fairbanks, have been run for decades, and in recent years other
short-distance races have begun in towns and villages throughout
the state. Alaska boasts more than one hundred organized
sled dog races, which run each year from November to April.

*Bristol
Bay*

ALASKA

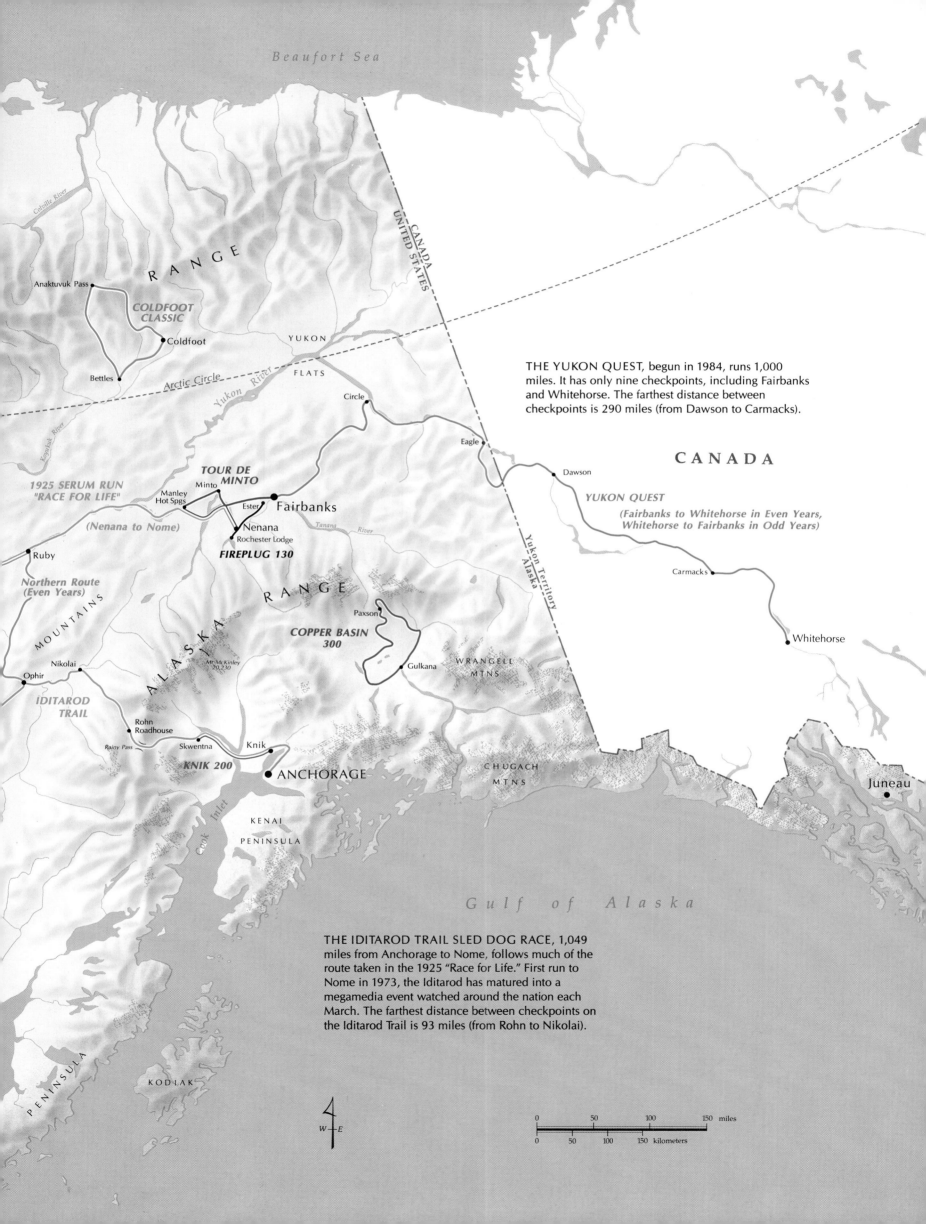

Beaufort Sea

Colville River

R A N G E

Anaktuvuk Pass

COLDFOOT
CLASSIC

Coldfoot

Bettles

Kobuk River

Arctic Circle

YUKON

FLATS

Yukon River

Circle

Eagle

CANADA
UNITED STATES

THE YUKON QUEST, begun in 1984, runs 1,000
miles. It has only nine checkpoints, including Fairbanks
and Whitehorse. The farthest distance between
checkpoints is 290 miles (from Dawson to Carmacks).

CANADA

Dawson

YUKON QUEST

(Fairbanks to Whitehorse in Even Years,
Whitehorse to Fairbanks in Odd Years)

1925 SERUM RUN
"RACE FOR LIFE"

TOUR DE
MINTO

Minto

Manley
Hot Spgs

Ester   Fairbanks

(Nenana to Nome)

Nenana
Rochester Lodge

FIREPLUG 130

Tanana River

Ruby

Northern Route
(Even Years)

Carmacks

M O U N T A I N S

A L A S K A   R A N G E

COPPER BASIN
300

Paxson

Whitehorse

Nikolai

*Mt. McKinley
20,230*

Gulkana

WRANGELL
MTNS

Yukon Territory
Alaska

Ophir

IDITAROD
TRAIL

Rohn
Roadhouse

Rainy Pass   Skwentna

Knik

KNIK 200   ● ANCHORAGE

CHUGACH
MTNS

Juneau

Cook Inlet

KENAI
PENINSULA

Gulf of Alaska

THE IDITAROD TRAIL SLED DOG RACE, 1,049
miles from Anchorage to Nome, follows much of the
route taken in the 1925 "Race for Life." First run to
Nome in 1973, the Iditarod has matured into a
megamedia event watched around the nation each
March. The farthest distance between checkpoints on
the Iditarod Trail is 93 miles (from Rohn to Nikolai).

P E N I N S U L A

KODIAK

W ─┼─ E

0   50   100   150   miles

0   50   100   150 kilometers

Father
of the
Iditarod

Ever since I was a youngster in Oklahoma reading Jack London's books, I knew I would come to Alaska to mush dogs. But I never imagined racing all over Alaska, or starting a race that would become an international event. The two things that please me most are that the Iditarod has become a national historic trail and the sled dog has been saved from extinction.

I remember visiting Unalakleet in the early 1950s and seeing a dog team behind every house. Everybody had a dog team because that was the only way you could get wood from the beach or water from the river. The only transportation was those dogs, and once every week, or every two weeks, or maybe only once a month, the mail plane would come in. Sled dogs were a way of life for those people. But when I returned in the 1960s, there was hardly a dog team around, and almost every house had a snow machine sitting in front of it. The snow machines did the work without needing to be fed in the summer. Other villages took longer to get snow machines than Unalakleet because they were less prosperous, but it was only a matter of time before snow machines were everywhere. Pretty soon, I was mushing supplies into DEW line sites in the Arctic, and none of those people up there had dog teams anymore. That was when I knew something had to be done to save the sled dog.

So we started a race. I knew the Iditarod Trail had been marked by gold stampeders headed north from Seward in 1908, and it was the only route into the Interior of Alaska until the 1920s. I homesteaded next to the trail in Knik. It made sense to me to use this old trail for a sled dog race.

But it took a lot of convincing. We formed a committee, and when I promised a race purse of fifty thousand dollars, people thought I was crazy. All but two of the committee members quit. But the race was a success, and at a banquet in a bar people asked, "What about next year?"

"You want another race?" I asked.

"Yes," they said.

"Okay, we'll give you another race." The rest is history.

The Iditarod means a lot to me. I have never won the race; I probably never will, but I have had some great experiences. I remember the year I left Rainy Pass in eighteenth place and passed everybody and came into Rohn in first place. I have never seen a team run as well as those dogs did. And I remember the night Joe Garnie and I traveled together down the Yukon River with the sky practically on fire with northern lights.

I am seventy-four now and figure I have traveled one hundred sixty thousand miles on a dogsled. I would like to reach two hundred thousand miles. There are lots of stories I enjoy telling to my grandchildren. And there are memorable times.

One of the most memorable was the spring of 1979 when I mushed a team of dogs to the summit of Mount McKinley, the highest mountain in North America. I was with guide Ray Genet, photographer Rob Stapleton, and Susan Butcher, who was then a young, aspiring musher. The expedition lasted forty days: thirty-eight to go up, and two to come down. We hit winds of a hundred miles an hour and temperatures of fifty below, but on May 28, when we reached the summit, Ray said it was the finest conditions he had seen in his twenty-seven times up there. The sky was clear, the temperature was eight degrees below zero, and there was no wind. We spent four hours on top. The dogs did great!

I am pleased to see so many people mushing dogs in Alaska these days. Most of it, I think, comes from the spirit of the Iditarod. Even the Fur Rendezvous World Championship Sled Dog Race was losing money and support when we started the Iditarod. It is doing much better now, and new races are born around the state every year. Dogsledding is a great sport, and the Iditarod Trail has a lot of magic. It has distance and history and difficult terrain. Some mushers today want to make the route easier, but I do not. It is a rough and rugged trail, but a good trail.

When I travel along that trail, I am traveling through some of the greatest history and landscape in Alaska, and it makes me feel mighty darn good. I have been first into almost every checkpoint along that race trail, except Nome. But I keep thinking . . . maybe next year. That is the Iditarod Spirit.

JOE REDINGTON, SR.

◄ *Joe Redington, Sr., "Father of the Iditarod," arrives in Unalakleet, in subzero temperatures during the Iditarod Trail Sled Dog Race.*

◄ Mike Madden's wheel dogs, Rocky and Dudley, wait in Unalakleet in a bitter cold coastal blizzard. Their destination is Nome, 269 miles away. At best, they will maintain a pace of ten to twelve mph. If the storm is too fierce to continue—which can happen along the Bering Sea Coast of the Seward Peninsula—they will curl up and wrap their tails across their faces. ▲ Kim Teasley drives across frozen Tolsona Lake at the beginning of the Copper Basin 300, near Glennallen.

▲ At 2:00 A.M. and -10°F, Joe Runyan arrives in the Athabascan village of Ruby on the Yukon River on the northern route of the Iditarod Trail Sled Dog Race. ▶ Rick Swenson shares the limelight with his lead dogs, Goose and Major, in Nome after winning his fifth Iditarod in 1991. One of the more memorable finishes, Swenson and second-place finisher Martin Buser battled a blizzard to reach Nome, while other front-runners waited in White Mountain.

CHAPTER ONE

Endurance,
Fidelity,
Intelligence

In the southeast corner of New York City's Central Park stands a bronze statue of a dog. Just an ordinary statue, perhaps, but not an ordinary dog. The eyes and ears are alert. The tail is up; the chest, forward. The dog faces north toward the Arctic, toward another time and another place. Most New Yorkers give it a glance and walk on. A few Sunday strollers stop.

Children climb onto the dog's back, as if mounting a horse, and grab the ears, which shine from the polishing of thousands of young hands that have been there before. Parents study the statue. They notice the dog is wearing a harness, and beneath its feet is an inscription that is difficult to read at first, but suddenly the words gain power, pulling the readers into another world where lives were saved and dogs were heroes. "Dedicated to the indomitable spirit of the sled dogs," it reads, "that relayed antitoxin six hundred miles over rough ice, across treacherous waters, through arctic blizzards from Nenana to the relief of stricken Nome in the winter of 1925. Endurance, Fidelity, Intelligence."

The readers stand back, and though the dog looks no different than it did before, it *is* different. It is alive, somehow, ready again to run to Nome and be the stuff of legends.

The dog's name is Balto. The legend goes like this: in late January 1925, Dr. Curtis Welch made several disturbing house calls in Nome, the gold-rush town anchored along the Seward Peninsula and frozen Bering Sea only 140 miles south of the Arctic Circle. Every patient he examined was weak, had a high fever, and experienced difficulty breathing. Most were children. Welch's worst fears were confirmed when he discovered the telltale false membranes in their throats and sinuses. It was diphtheria, a highly acute, contagious disease—and Nome had no serum.

Most of the town's seventeen hundred people were Eskimos, who were dangerously susceptible to white men's diseases. An epidemic seemed imminent. Dr. Welch called for help via the Army Signal Corps' radio relays, and enough serum was found a thousand miles away in Anchorage.

But how to get it there? Winter had settled down as cold as iron. Airplanes were a possibility. Only a year before, Carl Ben Eielson had flown the mail from Fairbanks to McGrath in his World War I Curtiss Jenny, signaling the beginning of the end of sled dog mail delivery in Alaska. But every plane in Alaska's Interior had been disassembled for winter storage, and short daylight hours made flying dangerous. If a plane went down, so would the serum. The next closest supply was in Seattle, weeks away. If Nome were to be saved, sled dog teams would have to do it.

The serum was loaded onto a special Alaska Railroad train in Anchorage and sent 250 miles north to Nenana, the end of the line on the Tanana River. Then began the "race for life" that, nearly fifty years later, would inspire the modern Iditarod Trail Sled Dog Race. The Northern Commercial Company had organized a relay of twenty freight mushers to carry the serum from Nenana to Nome, and there, waiting at the Nenana Train Station, was a Northern Commercial dog puncher named Wild Bill Shannon. Wasting no time, he took the twenty-pound package of serum, wrapped it in furs, tied it onto his sled, and turned his dog team down the frozen river. It was ten o'clock at night, January 27, 1925. The mercury had bottomed out at fifty degrees below zero.

About that same time, Leonhard Seppala, then the most famous dog musher in Alaska, drove his team out of Nome into a storm to meet the serum halfway. En route, he dropped dogs in Bluff where they would be well rested for the return trip to Nome. One of those dogs was Balto, now immortalized in New York's Central Park. While other mushers relayed the serum down the cold, quiet corridors of the Tanana and Yukon rivers, through places called Nine Mile, Whiskey Creek, Bishop Mountain, and Old Woman, Seppala battled a coastal blizzard with his most trusted dog, Togo, in the lead.

A tough Norwegian who had arrived in Nome in 1900, Seppala began driving dogs in 1901 and is widely credited with introducing Siberian huskies into the territory around 1908 to 1910. Most of his dogs were Siberians, including Balto and Togo, and with them he had won numerous races. Now he was racing against an epidemic, and every minute counted. To save time, he turned south at Isaac's Point, east of Golovin, and headed east across the frozen Norton

◄ *A bronze statue of Balto, the famous, life-saving sled dog, stands amid the colors of autumn in New York City's Central Park.*

Frosty-faced Jeff King arrives in Anvik.

Sound toward Unalakleet. There on the sea ice, he met Henry Ivanoff, who was traveling north from Shaktoolik with the serum in his sled. Seppala took the serum and headed back toward Golovin, ninety-one miles away. The temperature climbed, and he felt the sea ice shifting beneath him. At times, the wind blew so fiercely he could not see Togo up ahead through the blowing snow, yet Togo somehow knew where to go and found his way.

In Golovin, Seppala passed the serum to Charlie Olson, who made the howling, twenty-five-mile run to Bluff. Gunnar Kaasen then took the serum, harnessed up the dogs Seppala had dropped on the trip south, and headed for Port Safety with Balto in the lead. Twenty-two miles from Nome, Kaasen saw no lights in Port Safety, so he continued on. What happened next no one knows for certain—accounts vary—but one says that a gust of wind hit Kaasen so hard his sled blew over. The serum fell into the snow, and he had to dig it out with his bare hands.

On February 2, at 5:30 in the morning, Dr. Welch answered his door in Nome, thinking it was another report of diphtheria. "Instead," as one account says, "he saw an arctic apparition." There stood Gunnar Kaasen, his face caked in ice, his clothes covered with snow. He walked inside, handed Dr. Welch a package, and collapsed in a chair. In the package were three hundred thousand units of serum, frozen solid, but still good.

Nome was saved. Newspapers carried the story worldwide, and fame rained down on the twenty mushers and their teams who had carried the serum 674 miles in five days and seven hours. Balto and Togo lived in comfortable veneration from then on, and after their deaths, they were stuffed and put in museums. Leonhard Seppala, the consummate musher, logged a quarter of a million miles on his sled before his death in 1967, when his ashes were spread on the Iditarod Trail.

Though the legends never died, the Alaskan lifestyle and the sport of dogsledding nearly did. Alaska's two most famous sprint races, the Anchorage Fur Rendezvous World Championship and the Fairbanks Open North American, both begun in 1946, gained popularity through the years. But no major long-distance wilderness race had been run since the discontinuation of the All-Alaska Sweepstakes in 1917. The Iditarod Trail—called the Seward to Nome

Trail on old mail-carriers' maps—had not been traveled by dog team since the 1920s. Planes and snowmobiles had created new, faster modes of winter travel, and dogs were regarded as too slow and bothersome, loping along behind a changing world. A way of life was dying in Alaska. Sled dogs were passé.

That changed, of course, and how it happened deserves telling, for it is the story of one man's determination to keep a part of Alaska alive.

When the diphtheria serum arrived in Nome in the winter of 1925, Joe Redington was a seven-year-old boy working and playing in the dust of his father's Oklahoma homestead. His mother was an outlaw—rumored to be the daughter of Belle Starr, the notorious Bandit Queen—who one day rode away and never came back. Like the Joad family in Steinbeck's *Grapes of Wrath,* the Redingtons were down on their luck when the Great Depression hit in 1929, and the father, with Joe and his brother, pulled up stakes and headed for Anywhere, USA. They ended up harvesting wheat in Minnesota, banding turkeys in Wyoming, and picking fruit in California. A long, hard day's work would earn them a dollar each. They sold their Chrysler for thirteen dollars, jumped trains for a while—dodging railroad detectives—and finally arrived in Seattle in 1934 with their sights on Alaska. But the boat ticket north cost too much, and not until 1945 did the Redingtons cross the border into the Last Frontier. Someone put a husky puppy into the arms of twenty-eight-year-old Joe Redington, and then and there, a passion was born.

He homesteaded in Knik, north of Anchorage, and began to breed and raise dogs. He fished for a while, did some guiding, and ran a lodge with his wife, Vi. Then, with his dogs, he joined the Air Force Mountain Rescue to find downed planes on the slopes of nearby Mount Susitna. He loved being out with his dog team, and it perplexed him that so few other Alaskans even had teams. How could he resurrect this way of life? How could he save the sled dog from extinction? He opened some old books and maps, and an idea hit him: create a race along part of the route used by the serum mushers in 1925, splice it to the Iditarod Trail, run it more than a thousand miles from Anchorage to Nome, and call it the Iditarod Trail Sled Dog Race.

Signs in Ruby during the Iditarod Race

Critics howled. They could fathom sprint races of ten, twenty, and thirty miles. But a race of a thousand miles? Absurd. Other mushers said that without money and support for food and supplies, the dogs would starve to death, and even with support, they would probably not have the stamina for such a race. Newspapers labeled Redington a northern Don Quixote, a dreamer. Undaunted, he pushed on, and not even Nostradamus could have prophesied the fruits of his labors. At first, only a few joined him in his dream, the most significant among them an amateur historian from Wasilla named Dorothy Page.

The first Anchorage-to-Nome Iditarod Trail Sled Dog Race was run in 1973. Redington had promised a purse of fifty thousand dollars to the finishing mushers in Nome, but the night before the race began, his bank account was empty. While thirty-four dog teams started, Redington himself stayed behind to raise money and coordinate supply flights along the trail.

Victory that year went to Dick Wilmarth, who arrived in Nome in twenty days and claimed a winner's prize of twelve thousand dollars. Redington had raised the prize money, Alaskans were charmed by the outrageous event, and the Iditarod—the "Last Great Race on Earth"—was born.

Thirty dogs died on the trail that year. Today, an average of one or two is lost each race—not bad, considering that more than fourteen hundred run, and the race is nearly twice as fast as it was in 1973. Each dog is examined by a veterinarian before the race begins, and again at checkpoints along the way.

Any long-time musher will tell you the quality of dog care in Alaska has soared since 1973, and with it, the knowledge of dog physiology, breeding, and diet. The village dog of yesteryear, the little Alaskan husky, has become the best marathon runner in the world. Bred and trained to trot more than one hundred miles a day on tough feet, with a strong appetite and a good attitude—the willingness to pull, pull, and pull—the Alaskan husky has not only emerged from the shadow of the snow machine, but it has also stolen the hearts and imaginations of people everywhere.

Joe Redington, Sr., should know; he has more than four hundred of them in his kennel in Knik. Every serious long-distance musher in Alaska has, at one time or another, purchased, borrowed, or bred huskies from Redington. More than half the dogs in any Iditarod Race are either directly from his kennel or descended from it. Part entrepreneur, part philanthropist, Redington will share his dogs—and his knowledge—with almost anyone who asks.

"German shepherds are good workers and have tough feet," he once told the *Anchorage Daily News,* "but they're too heavy-boned and have neither speed nor endurance. Purebred Doberman pinschers are too smart. They look like they're working when they're not. And at least the ones I had were so mean the huskies wouldn't breed with them, so I never got any crosses. Samoyeds have enough speed but no endurance, no matter how you train them. Ten or twelve miles is their maximum. And they have a long-fur problem. Their feet ball up easily. Norwegian elkhounds are slow and bark a lot. I never tried salukis or borzois or Russian wolfhounds or greyhounds because I'd heard old-timers say that crosses with any of them never worked out. Generally, their backs wouldn't hold up under the pulling."

The Alaskan malamute, used as a freight-hauling dog by coastal Eskimos and turn-of-the-century prospectors, is too big and slow for long-distance racing. Whereas the malamute weighs seventy to ninety pounds, the fleet-footed Alaskan husky weighs only thirty-five to fifty-five pounds.

And what of the Siberian husky, used in the 1925 diphtheria serum run and favored by Leonhard Seppala and other early long-distance mushers? "A Siberian husky is more of a sensitive dog," says Redington. "He has real good feet, a good coat, and they're good to breed into because you get a lot of good characteristics. But they're poor eaters when under stress. And they're not the dog for the Iditarod by any means."

The dog for the Iditarod is the Alaskan husky, a small, mixed breed native to the Athabascan villages of the Interior. And it is the dog for short-distance races as well. Decades of breeding experiments have given it great speed and stamina, along with mental and physical toughness, but it has also developed a random outward appearance that has cost it recognition as a pure breed. According to the American Kennel Club, the Alaskan husky does not exist. But according to mushers far and wide, no heart beats stronger and more true than that inside the Alaskan husky.

Two Alaskan huskies wait to race in Fairbanks.

"It's very simple—there's no opinion on it," says veteran musher and author Jim Welch. "The dog either does it or not. That's the beauty of a race, as opposed to a dog show. And at the end of the race, the team with the best time wins—not the team that appealed most to the judge because of the color of the suit the handler was wearing, or the political influence the owner had with the judges. You can't influence the clock. It's a standard that's fair for everybody."

Leonhard Seppala would be amazed. A sport he enjoyed in its infancy has now entered its adolescence, maturing into a serious enterprise for an increasing number of Alaskans. Back-lot mushers of a few years ago are avid students of Mendelian genetics today. They breed this dog to that one, that dog to this one, keeping log books and medical charts, aiming for speed, attitude, and durability. And getting it.

Race records are broken every year, veterinary care has soared, and—best of all—dogs across Alaska are treated with more kindness and respect than ever before. "You need me; I need you," is the credo between musher and dogs. They are a coach and a team—a family.

So you want to become a full-time professional dog musher? Consider this. A healthy husky will cost about eight hundred dollars a year in food and veterinary care. A strong kennel has at least thirty dogs; the strongest, upwards of one hundred, or even more.

Equipment can run into tens of thousands of dollars, sponsors are tough to get, and races are hard to win. If you want to purchase a trained, experienced lead dog from a well-known musher, plan on spending at least fifteen hundred dollars. An entire team of well-bred, trained, and experienced dogs could cost from ten to twenty thousand dollars. Long gone are the days when you could buy forty or fifty good huskies from kennels on the Yukon River for a hundred dollars per dog. Gone, too, are the days when recreational mushers won major races. This is serious business for serious money.

In recent years, sled dog races have popped up across Alaska as fast as fireweed. There is the 1000-mile Yukon Quest International between Fairbanks and Whitehorse, the toughest race of them all, some mushers say; the Kuskokwim 300 from Bethel to Aniak and back, honoring the 1906 sled dog mail route pioneered on the Kuskokwim River by musher Oscar Samuelson and his son John; the Copper Basin 300 along the volcanic Wrangell Mountains; the Coldfoot Classic through Gates of the Arctic National Park, discontinued but not without hope that it will someday run again; the Tour de Minto; the Su Valley 300; the Fireplug 130; and many more.

Short-distance races have proliferated as well, with those in Anchorage and Fairbanks offering the greatest winnings. But it is the fun races in remote villages that likely offer the strongest sense of history, family, and place, for here young Athabascans and Eskimos can again travel by dog team through the great white silence as their ancestors did, free from the tension and noise of the modern, hyperactive world.

More than a hundred organized sled dog races are now run each year in Alaska, many of them inspired one way or another by the Iditarod. Not only has the sled dog been saved from extinction—as Redington desired—it has also become a bright-eyed symbol of the Alaskan spirit.

In April 1991, a handful of mushers carried that spirit with them to the Soviet Union, traveling by dog team from Nome up the coast of the Seward Peninsula to Wales. From there, they flew by plane across the Bering Strait to Uelen in the Soviet Far East and continued to mush to the Chukotka mining city of Anadyr, a thousand miles from Nome.

It was no ordinary race. In fact, it was not a race at all. There was no entrance fee nor winner's purse. They called it the Hope 91, and they traveled in cooperation, not competition, to celebrate a better, brighter world of newfound friendship across the shores of the "divided twins." Gifts were exchanged and stories told, as Alaskan and Soviet mushers traveled the trail side by side and discovered that the same qualities that saved Nome long ago—endurance, fidelity, and intelligence—can save the world today.

▶ *A litter of six-week-old Alaskan huskies—future sled dogs—learns the ropes on a sled in Moose Meadow, Girdwood, Alaska.*

◄ Octogenarian Norman Vaughan, the oldest musher to run the Iditarod, arrives in Rohn en route, once again, to Nome. ▲ Backdropped by 12,010-foot Mount Drum, Mark Weber drives his team down the frozen Gulkana River during the Copper Basin 300 Sled Dog Race. ►► In the treacherous Dalzell Gorge, between Rainy Pass and the Rohn checkpoint, Bill Cotter mushes his team over open water on a makeshift bridge of spruce logs, bows, and snow.

▲ In White Mountain, small speed sleds await front-running mushers who will switch to them for the final seventy-seven miles to Nome on the Iditarod Trail Sled Dog Race.   ▶ Nenana trapper Charlie Boulding changes runners on his overturned sled in Circle during the thousand-mile Yukon Quest International Sled Dog Race.   ▶▶ En route from Shungnak to Ambler near the Arctic Circle, Ed Iten crosses the Kobuk River during the Kobuk 440 Sled Dog Race.

◄ Lorraine Temple, owner of the Homer-based Outback Kachemak Dog Sled Tours, talks with two-month-old Chester, an Alaskan husky and—hopefully— a future lead dog on Lorraine's team. In summer, Lorraine works as a boat skipper in Kachemak Bay, Kenai Fjords, and Prince William Sound. ▲ Bruce Johnson drives his team north along the Trans-Alaska Oil Pipeline, during the Copper Basin 300 Sled Dog Race, which is run each year in January.

▲ Alexander "Sasha" Reznyuk, one of two Russians to first run the Iditarod (after training with Joe Redington, Sr., in the winter of 1990-91) departs Wasilla during the restart of the race. Ahead lay more than a thousand miles of snowy, icy, rocky trail to Nome. ▶ Greg Jefferies wears an icy beard after mushing eight miles through -15° F weather during the Orville Lake Memorial Sled Dog Race, at the Tudor Track in Anchorage. Jefferies finished first in the seven-dog class.

◄ Villagers and members of the media gather at dusk in White Mountain to watch Iditarod champion Susan Butcher prepare a small speed sled for her final dash to Nome, seventy-seven miles away. A six-hour mandatory layover here helps to prevent mushers from pushing their dogs too hard as they approach the finish line.   ▲ Gear hangs to dry from the rafters of the one-room cabin in Rohn, as rookie musher Bert Hanson catches some sleep in the corner.

▲ Emmitt Peters, the "Yukon Fox" and winner of the 1975 Iditarod, prepares a meal for his dogs in Rohn. Most competitive mushers feed their dogs a "high octane" commercial dog food supplemented with various amounts of meat and fat. The meat protein helps to alleviate stress; the fat, to alleviate cold. ▶ With a name and face out of a Jack London novel, Buck, a wheel dog belonging to Kevin Kerns, rests near Glennallen during the Copper Basin 300 Sled Dog Race.

THE IDITAROD

SEWARD PENINSULA

NOME
22 Safety
55 White Mountain
18 Golovin
28 Elim
Koyuk
48
58

Norton Sound

⊶ Race Checkpoint

89 Approximate distance (in miles)
between Checkpoints

Race routes are generalized where
they follow river courses.

0   25   50   75   100 miles
0   25   50   75   100   150 kilometers

Elevations in feet

Shaktoolik
40
Unalakleet
90
Kaltag
42
70
Eagle Island
60
Grayling
18
Anvik
25
Shageluk
65
Iditarod
90
Southern Route
(Odd Years)

NULATO HILLS

Nulato
Northern Route
(Even Years)
52
Galena
52
Ruby
75
Sultatna
Crossing
45
Cripple
60
Ophir
38
Takotna
23
McGrath
48
Nikolai

KOKRINES HILLS

YUKON RIVER

MOUNTAINS

KUSKOKWIM

93
Rohn
Roadhouse
48
Rainy
Pass
30
Finger Lake
45
Skwentna

ALASKA RANGE

Mt McKinley

88

Knik 14 Wasilla

ANCHORAGE
20
Eagle River

KENAI
PENINSULA

Cook Inlet

CHAPTER TWO

The Last
Great Race
on Earth

And so it begins. On a brisk morning in late winter, amid a wild, cheering crowd packed on Fourth Avenue in downtown Anchorage, seventy-five mushers and fifteen hundred huskies line up for the grandest of all Alaskan sporting events: the Iditarod Trail Sled Dog Race to Nome. Banners flutter in the wind. Bundled children sit atop parents' shoulders. The dogs bark wildly and jump straight up in their harnesses. The mushers make last-minute preparations. Gear on, sleds loaded, dogs harnessed, handlers ready. The noise is incredible—the cheering, the barking, the voice on the loudspeaker . . . "Ladies and gentlemen . . . welcome to the Last Great Race on Earth."

Sunrise spills onto the snowy avenue. It is nine o'clock. The first team comes to the line with twenty huskies straining forward. Countdown. ". . . Five, four, three, two, one, GO!" They're off. Every calorie invested in barking and jumping suddenly converts into forward motion as the dogs bolt down the avenue with tongues out and snow flying about their paws. Another team takes off, then another, charging ahead in two-minute intervals, racing through Anchorage to Eagle River, past thousands of clapping, mittened hands, eventually slowing to a steady trot for the long journey northwest to Nome, following frozen rivers and historic trails for more than a thousand miles. Behind each team are years of training, breeding, feeding, and tens of thousands of dollars in expenses; ahead are two weeks of sleeplessness, physical exhaustion, bitter cold, strong winds, and silent travel through the magnificent, unforgiving wilds of Alaska.

This is more than a sporting event; it is an epic. Alaskan newspapers, television, and radio stations will shove aside the Persian Gulf and perestroika to give the Iditarod equal attention, if not more. ABC's "Wide World of Sports" will bring the race into millions of homes nationwide.

Each team can begin with as many as twenty dogs in harness, and must finish with at least five. Those dogs unable to finish will be "dropped" at checkpoints and returned to the musher after the race.

If the weather and trail conditions are good, the winner will reach Nome in eleven days. If storms roll in, it could take twice that long. Be it eleven days or twenty, across the state, Alaskans will set aside a part of each day to vicariously live the struggles and strategies of the seventy-five sled dog teams racing through winter's cold, reaffirming in a world of fax machines and missiles that there is more to life than increasing its speed, that you can win a victory just by being there with the dogs and the cold and the northern lights. Ask the man in the business suit standing on Cordova Street watching the teams go by. He is an overworked accountant headed for his Anchorage office, and he holds a briefcase with a sticker on it that says, "I'd rather be running the Iditarod."

Would he really?

It is hardly a vacation. The dogs will burn eight thousand calories per day, and before the race ends, the mushers will lose five or ten pounds each. Some will fall asleep on their sleds. Some will fall asleep and *off* their sleds. Some will run into trees. Others will be blown over by the wind. Some will get lost. Some will get hurt. Some will get frostbite on their faces and hands. A few will scratch (fail to finish), and more than one will hallucinate on the trail and see swords falling from the sky, or trees turning into sharks' teeth. Yet all will tell you that running the Iditarod beats doing taxes.

And a few will run flawlessly.

"There's nothing quite like the Iditarod in all the world, if you ask me," wrote musher and sports writer Tim Mowry in the *Fairbanks Daily News Miner.* "It's as if you're on another planet for two weeks out of the year and come back to Earth for the remaining fifty. If I ever write a book, it will read, 'Life is boring after you run the Iditarod.'"

After running twenty miles from downtown Anchorage to Eagle River, the teams are loaded into trucks and driven to Wasilla for a restart. From there, the race follows the Knik-Goose Bay Road to Knik, then leaves civilization and heads across wilderness Alaska for Skwentna, Finger Lake, and points north. The farther into the race, the more the mushers spread out, and soon the Iditarod becomes three races: one among the front-runners to win, one among the middle-runners to finish respectably, and one among the back-runners to finish, period.

About 260 miles down the trail, they cross the Alaska Range at Rainy Pass, then drop into the Dalzell Gorge before arriving at the Rohn Roadhouse, where the Tatina River joins the South Fork of

Dogsledding enthusiasm in Delta Junction

the Kuskokwim River. The trail climbs and falls, twists and winds, and the mushers—especially the less-experienced ones—hang on for dear life. The wind and blowing snow can be blinding, open water can appear in the gorge, and the air can get as cold as steel, for this is Interior Alaska—north of the mountains—and there is little room for carelessness and mistakes.

Ahead lies the Farewell Burn, an easy place to get lost amid a vast stand of ghostlike spruce burned long ago in a fire. Then comes Nikolai, the first Native village on the trail, and McGrath, a town of five hundred on the confluence of the Kuskokwim and Takotna rivers. Most of the mushers take their twenty-four-hour mandatory layover in Rohn, Nikolai, or McGrath. Townsfolk turn out to greet them at any hour, and hospitality abounds. Listed on a wall in McGrath are the names of families who have invited mushers for a home-cooked meal, a hot shower, and a soft bed.

In Ophir, sixty-one miles north of McGrath, the trail splits into a northern route, which the race follows in even-numbered years, and a southern route, which it follows in odd-numbered years. Though the official distance of the race is 1,049 miles (1,000 because it is at least that long, and 49 because Alaska is the 49th state), the actual race distances are approximately 1,158 miles by the northern route and 1,163 miles by the southern route.

The first musher to the halfway point (Cripple Landing on the northern route, the ghost town of Iditarod on the southern) wins a pot of specially-minted silver ingots but also gets jinxed, for seldom does he or she win the race.

The town of Iditarod sits quietly between the Yukon River and the Kuskokwim Mountains in a land the Ingalik Indians called "Haiditarod," meaning a far, distant place. Not too far and distant for two prospectors, however, who, on Christmas Day 1908, picked their way through the frozen gravel of Otter Creek and discovered gold. They promised to keep it a secret, which must have lasted about a week, for two years later Iditarod was a bustling town of ten thousand drifters, gamblers, hookers, merchants, and miners, including two dentists, two tobacconists, six lawyers, and an undertaker. Most of them arrived by steamship up the Yukon River, or by foot or dogsled overland from Seward, through the Alaska Range, and along what is today called the Iditarod Trail.

Dogsledding was a winter way of life in Iditarod, and famous freight mushers like the Malemute Kid and John "Iron Man" Johnson soon came to town. By 1911, local races were commonplace, with wagers running high and spirits higher. But three years later, the gold played out, and the boom turned to bust. Only one person called Iditarod home in 1940. No one calls it that today. The trail itself was used for a few years after the gold rush to carry mail and supplies into Interior Alaska and Nome, and it has since been designated a U.S. National Historic Trail. But the town itself is still a far, distant place, and the most action it ever sees now is every other March during the Iditarod Trail Sled Dog Race.

Farther on, the race arrives at the mighty Yukon River (at the village of Ruby on the northern route; at Anvik on the southern) where a seven-course dinner is prepared and served for the first musher. And this time, there is no jinx.

One race strategy is to get out front as early as possible, running your dogs on a precise timetable of work and rest, hoping to distance yourself so no one can catch you. If a storm traps the pack farther back, victory is yours. Joe May did this in 1980 and won. Others have tried the same thing, however, and lost. Leading has its disadvantages: your dogs must work harder to find a trail, since there is no scent from previous teams; you risk encounters with moose and open water; and one improper trail marker might send you the wrong direction. This happened to Joe Garnie in 1986 when he went awry for forty miles, lost his lead and valuable time, and finished in second place, five hours behind winner Susan Butcher.

Another strategy is to let someone else lead while always staying in striking distance. Rick Swenson, who has the fastest average finishing time of any Iditarod musher, excels at this. Preying on the impatience of others as they approach Nome, he lets them charge into bitter winds off the frozen Bering Sea, and then, with their teams numbed and tired and resting, he glides by to victory. Not always, however, for others have done the same thing to him.

No single musher has a patent on new strategies. Whenever someone comes along with an idea—like Joe Runyan in 1989 when he broke Susan Butcher's winning streak by combining long running and resting times—several other mushers will try that idea the next year.

Dalton, an Alaskan husky, waits to run in Wasilla.

The front-runners study each other. Whose dogs are tight in their harnesses? Whose are loping? Whose are drinking and eating well? Whose are drinking and eating poorly? Who is losing momentum? Who is gaining it?

They notice the details of each other's teams. Dogs with diarrhea could indicate fatigue, poor diet, or a viral infection. They listen to their radios for trail and weather reports. There are friendship and camaraderie and long hours on the trail together, but also serious competition. They pretend to fall asleep at a checkpoint, then get up and leave. They sleep in secretive places and keep alarms in their wool hats so others will not hear them go off. They tell the press one thing, and then they do something else. They invent misinformation and spread it around to deceive other mushers into changing their strategies and schedules. Sometimes it works; sometimes it does not. Whatever the strategy, it is seldom enough, in itself, to win. Good physical conditioning of both musher and dogs is essential, and the weather is always a wild card.

For the 1991 Iditarod, Susan Butcher had trained a long-distance dog team many mushers believed was the finest ever assembled. She consistently posted the best running times between checkpoints. It was her race. "Do her dogs look as good as they always do?" asked her chief rival, Rick Swenson, as he passed through Elim thirty minutes behind her. Everyone nodded. But seventy miles from Nome, Butcher hit an arctic blizzard and turned around in blinding, blowing snow while Swenson, hungry for an Iditarod victory after nine years without one, pressed on. "Rick is either going to win this race or die out there," said musher Tim Osmar as he waited out the storm with Butcher in White Mountain. Twenty-eight hours later, a weary Swenson emerged victorious in Nome. Martin Buser finished second; Susan Butcher, third. The weather had played its hand, and grit, not strategy, had determined the winner.

The same thing happened in 1985, the memorable year Libby Riddles mushed out of Shaktoolik and into a storm while the rest of the front-runners waited. Surely she would turn back, they all thought. So they waited, and waited. No Libby. Soon, it became obvious that the twenty-eight-year-old woman from Teller was either in trouble or going to win. And win she did. Hearts were captured around the nation when she mushed into Nome, and the Iditarod Trail Sled Dog Race has never been the same since.

Now there is an official truck of the Iditarod; an official beer of the Iditarod; and an official footwear, dog food, snack food, bank, airline, and hotel of the Iditarod. Corporate America has arrived. Well-known Iditarod mushers once wore the drab-but-functional winter gear typical of backcountry life in Alaska's bush. Today, they look like rainbows in their fancy, patch-covered, color-coordinated, high-tech clothing, courtesy of large sponsors. For occupations, they list sales manager, fisherman, school teacher, miner, printer, trapper, mechanic, lawyer, bartender, businessman, veterinarian, plumber, doctor, carpenter, wilderness guide, or—every so often—"full-time dog breeder and dog musher." But for sponsors, they list a growing panoply of American big business.

Most mushers are Alaskans, but a few come from Japan, Europe, Canada, the Soviet Union, and the Lower 48. Terry Hinesly, a probation officer and member of the Sports Car Club of America, has trained at the Oregon Dune Mushers Mail Run, a sled dog race across eighty miles of sand. Two Russians, Nikoli Ettyne and Alexander Reznyuk, trained in Knik with Joe Redington, Sr., the "Father of the Iditarod," before running the race. Roy and Leslie Monk, a husband-wife team from England, made a wager with each other that "the last one to Nome will do the dishes for the next six months." Both scratched.

There is disappointment and heartache, inspiration and pride, surprise and boredom, fear and loathing, fun and friendship—and love. A love for the Iditarod so infected Swiss-born musher Martin Buser and his wife, Kathy, that they named their two sons, Nikolai and Rohn, after checkpoints on the trail. And Beverly Jerue, an Athabascan who began competitive dog sledding in 1979, fell in love not only with the Iditarod, but with another musher as well, Jan Masek, whom she married on the trail in 1984. Now when the race brings her through her childhood home of Anvik, her uncle rings the church bell, and the entire town—nearly ninety people, many of whom are her relatives—turns out to greet her.

So it goes on the Iditarod Trail. The northern and southern routes converge at the village of Kaltag, on the Yukon River, and the trail heads overland ninety miles to the Eskimo settlement of Unalakleet,

Someday my day will come.

on the frozen shore of the Bering Sea. Ahead lie the final 270 miles to Nome, often the longest, most bitter, most difficult miles. "Whoever gets to the coast early and with the strongest dogs has the best shot at victory," Rick Swenson once said. Up the coast to Shaktoolik; across frozen Norton Sound to Koyuk; west to Elim, Golovin, and White Mountain; over the Topkok Hills, the teams push on. Many top mushers train on this stretch prior to the race, familiarizing their dogs with the trail, instilling in them a "homing instinct" for Nome.

The drama builds; bets are made; speculation abounds. Everyone has his or her favorite musher, whether anyone admits it or not.

Just as colorful as the front of the race are the stories that unfold among mushers far back in the pack, sometimes all the way back. Here, for example, you will find octogenarian Colonel Norman Vaughan, vice president of the Greenland Expedition Society. He accompanied Richard E. Byrd to Antarctica in 1928 to 1930, competed in the Winter Olympics in 1932, took 209 sled dogs and 17 mushers to the Battle of the Bulge during World War II, and came to Alaska in 1978 with hardly a penny to his name. On New Year's Eve 1987, at age 82, he married Carolyn Muegge, who, the year before, had mushed with him on the Iditarod. "It truly is the last great race on earth," he says of the Iditarod. He should know. In 1990, he raced in his twelfth Iditarod to raise money for the Alaska chapter of The Nature Conservancy. Donations were pledged for every mile he covered, and he made it all the way to Nome. Others have raced to raise money for research in muscular dystrophy and AIDS; to support abused children, the homeless, and American prisoners of war.

The Iditarod has changed and will continue to change. The world is watching now, the rules have tightened, and the regulation book has grown. Some mushers pine for the old days of anonymity, when stories were told late into the night and the Iditarod was more of a two-week camping trip than a race. But most welcome the attention, and with it the improved treatment of sled dogs across Alaska. The ranks of race volunteers—checkers, veterinarians, trailbreakers, judges, logistics coordinators, telephone operators, ham radio operators, and dozens of pilots with their own planes (called the Iditarod Air Force)—have swelled into the hundreds. Now, helicopters hover over the front-runners with cameramen hanging out the doors. And journalists wait like a hungry pack at the next checkpoint to pounce on the first musher who arrives. A dozen microphones appear, and suddenly a musher who has traveled all day and half the night is expected to say something profound.

"How was the trail?"

"Rough."

"How do you feel?"

"Cold."

"How are your dogs?"

"Tired."

"Are you worried about Swenson?"

"No."

"Can you maintain this pace?"

"Yes."

"Is Butcher beatable?"

"Maybe."

The checker makes sure the musher has the required gear in his or her sled—axe, sleeping bag, snowshoes, dog food, dog booties, and mail packet—while local villagers gather around the frosty-faced dogs that roll in the snow. The children watch with wide-eyed wonder, hoping, perhaps, to ask a question or catch a smile from the musher who stands as tall to them as Joe Montana or Magic Johnson does to children down south.

They remember Joe Runyan giving them a piece of candy, or Jerry Austin letting them pet his lead dog, or Dee Dee Jonrowe laughing aloud. They remember the famous names in the middle of the night, the eyelashes covered with frost, the faces lighted by camera strobes, the magnetism between musher and dogs. They remember it all, the magical stuff of dreams and ambitions.

Twenty years later, the race will belong to them. They will be the next generation of Iditarod spectators, volunteers, and mushers, crossing the Great Land en route to Nome, carrying with them the hearts and imaginations of thousands. And they, too, might find the time to stop in a remote village, pull a piece of candy from their sled bag, and give it to a smiling, dream-filled child.

► *The Iditarod begins on Fourth Avenue, Anchorage.* ► ► *Sunrise captures an Iditarod musher on the Yukon River, near Ruby.*

◄ A crowd gathers in Fairbanks in late February, on the frozen Chena River, to watch the start of the Yukon Quest International Sled Dog Race, a thousand-mile epic journey to Whitehorse in Canada's Yukon Territory. In alternate years, the race runs the other way, beginning in Whitehorse and ending in Fairbanks.
▲ In early April sunshine that looks warmer than it really is, Jacques Philip drives his team down the Kobuk River during the Kobuk 440 Sled Dog Race.

▲ Becky Sather's lead dogs, Pilot and Midnight, rest in subzero temperatures at Circle Hot Springs, during the Yukon Quest. Generally, the worse the trail conditions—strong winds, cold temperatures, deep snow—the more rest a team requires.   ▶ Kate Persons arrives in Ambler with a frosty face at -20°F during the Kobuk 440. In April, 1991, she was the first musher to complete the Alaska-Chukotka Great Race run from Nome, Alaska, to Anadyr in the Soviet Far East.

◄ Fudge, a seven-year-old male husky, rests on top of his dog house in the June heat in Denali National Park. Since the 1920s, sled dogs have been used for winter patrols in the park. ▲ Iditarod champion Rick Swenson trains his sled dogs using an all-terrain vehicle amid autumn-colored aspens in Two Rivers, near Fairbanks. ► ► A crowd watches Chuck Erhart drive his team down Fairbank's Second Avenue during the Open North American Sled Dog Race.

▲ Greg Probst "skijors" behind Jennifer Wolk as she mushes her team along the north boundary of Denali National Park. ▶ Tuglines, necklines, and a gangline lay atop a new sled bag belonging to Iditarod champion Susan Butcher. ▶ ▶ Two-month-old husky puppies, Chester, Woody, and Critter, rest on a dogsled while their littermate, Bo, chews on a line. At age six to eight months, they will begin training in harness, pulling light loads for only a mile or two.

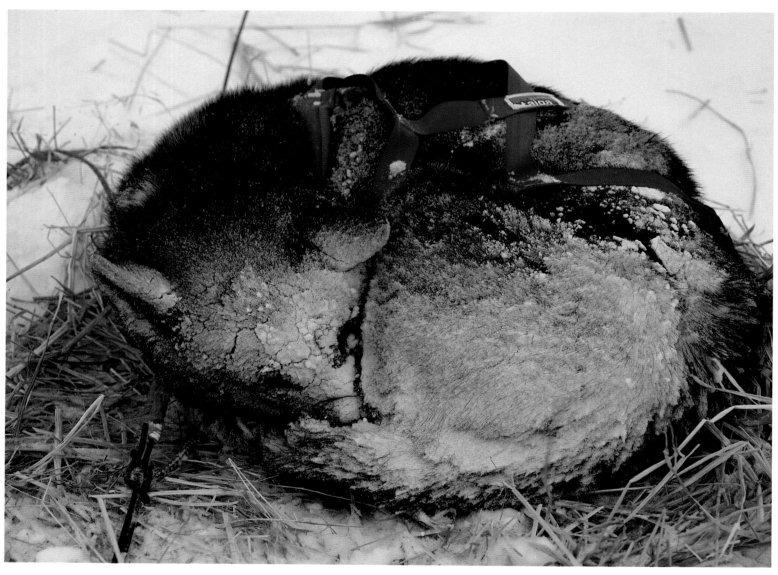

▲ A frosted Alaskan husky belonging to musher Peryll Kyzer curls up in a storm in Unalakleet during the Iditarod Trail Sled Dog Race. Although the dog might appear cold, it is not; frostbite is rare among huskies preadapted to the north. ▶ Fatigued and lightly frostbitten after battling a storm for twenty-four hours with wind chills to -50°F, Martin Buser arrives in Nome at 3:30 in the morning for a second-place finish in the Iditarod Trail Sled Dog Race.

CHAPTER THREE

Forty Below
and
Forty to Go

It is forty degrees below zero, and you have forty miles to go to a warm cabin. Forty miles, not by truck, train, boat, or plane, but by sled dog team. Slow going. The night is clear, yet a strong wind has blown snowdrifts over the trail. The dogs trudge ahead at five miles an hour, moving through the blackness with booties on their feet and frost on their faces.

In the lead is Kanuti, your best dog, the dog you would do 'most anything for because he once did the same for you—risked his life to save yours—and a dog like that comes along only once in a lifetime, if ever. The rest of the team follows, nine dogs in all. Their breathing dances in the light from your headlamp, the only light around, save for a million stars overhead. Orion, Pegasus, and the Pleiades shine through the air with mesmerizing clarity. You stare at them as the sled jostles forward on the lonely trail, sinking into the dark distance over ice and snow on this beautiful, dangerous night.

You are on the Yukon River, Alaska's largest winter artery, moving east toward Crazy Creek, where a cabin rests in the woods and your buddies wait with hot moose stew on the stove. Crazy Creek. They say a man went crazy there once. Spent too much time alone and shot himself. He was found in the spring frozen stiff with a note beside him that said, "Better to die from a bullet than from the cold." Until then, no one knew he could even write.

Exhausted, you drift into random thoughts: hot moose stew, Dutch apple pie, money, love, living, dying. Is it truly better to shoot yourself than to freeze to death? A chill runs down your spine. The air is cold enough to make your teeth ache. Ice cakes your moustache. Frostbite gnaws at your fingers. The dogs keep moving. Onward.

They say freezing is like falling asleep. Once the panic and pain subside, you just drift away. Not so bad after all. You reach inside the sled bag for your gun. It is there, tucked between your snowshoes and sleeping bag. It feels awkward through the thick layers of your mittens. You have carried a gun ever since your team ran into

a moose on the trail and two dogs were kicked and badly injured. That was before Kanuti was born.

Lazy Kanuti, you called him as a pup, the little husky that showed absolutely no promise as a sled dog. But some dogs, like some people, are late bloomers, and so it was with Kanuti. As he aged, he matured. You ran him every day. His feet grew tough; his heart, strong; his devotion, deep. Then he developed that rare sixth sense that makes a great lead dog and carries a team through a blinding storm. Now in mid-trot, he turns his head to check on the rest of the team, and he sees you slumped back onto the handlebar of the sled, sound asleep with a safety rope around your waist.

You dream about the cabin up ahead and your buddies inside. They are laughing and playing cards and warming their backs to a fire, while you are out here in the cold, alone amid what Robert Service called "the great white silence," marking the map's void spaces, mingling with the mongrel races. Crazy fool. Every year you say you are going to spend the winter in Hawaii or in the Bahamas, and every winter you stay right here and mush dogs. What is wrong with you? Are you maybe a little old for this? Fifty-six and "fit as a fiddle," your doctor said after your last check-up. But you are asleep on your sled on the Yukon River, your dogs are as tired as you are, and it is forty degrees below zero. Wake up!

Not even Kanuti sees the danger coming. The wind has buried the trail in some places, scoured it in others. The embankment is a shelf of steeply sloping ice above open water, and the sled is sliding toward it. Kanuti turns upslope, and the team follows, but there is no fresh snow for traction. They slip. The sled rattles across the ice and falls to its side, taking you with it. You hit hard; there is a loud snap. Your left arm has slipped through your waist rope and is now pinned against your side. Your other arm lies trapped under the overturned sled. In three seconds, your feet are burning from the needle-like pain of freezing river water flooding your boots. Five seconds later, you are wet to your knees. Using the arm under the sled, you try to pull yourself forward. A pain shoots through you; the arm is broken.

With a little slack between you and the sled, you could free your good arm and pull yourself up. You try to move but cannot. The dogs stand as still as stone on the icy slope, afraid to move forward

◀ *Backdropped by late January alpenglow, a lone musher travels between Chistochina and Summit Lake in the Copper Basin 300.*

61

A husky endures a storm on the Bering Sea Coast.

for fear of slipping back, their feet providing just enough traction to keep the sled, and you, from sliding deeper into the water. They try again to move up the slope but cannot; it is too icy and steep. You search for solutions, but already the cold has muddled your mind. The snow hook is out of reach. You hear a clattering and realize it is your teeth. The water climbs up your thighs and freezes.

You flash your headlamp ahead and see a lone spruce tree directly to the right of the team.

"Gee," you yell, but the words come out in a throaty mumble. You can hardly work your mouth.

"Gee, Kanuti, GEE!"

Kanuti moves to the right. The swing dogs follow. They slip, and the sled moves back. The dogs stop.

"GEE, KANUTI."

As if he suddenly realizes what you are trying to do, Kanuti aims for the spruce and pulls at an angle with all his might, taking the team with him until the gangline wraps around the tree at ninety degrees. Now you have an anchor.

"Let's go, Kanuti. Let's go."

The team advances and the sled inches upslope. A bit farther and they can advance no more because the neckline of one dog has tightened against the tree. But you are far enough out of the water to lift a frozen leg, push against the ice, and create some slack in the rope around your waist. Your good arm comes free. Now you have a fighting chance. Your heart pounds. There is a surge of adrenaline as you grab the loaded, three-hundred-pound sled and lift. The broken arm comes free.

You feel nothing from your knees down; your lower legs might as well be iron. But you feel no pain, either. On your feet, you lift the sled onto its runners and push.

"Haw, Kanuti, haw."

Kanuti turns to the left and heads upslope, groping for solid footing on packed snow. He finds some. The sled moves forward. In less than a minute, you are back on solid ground. There is no time to waste. With one good arm you set the snow hook, open your sled bag, throw out some gear and toss a frozen sheefish to each dog. You unharness Kanuti and bring him to the sled, then kick your feet and legs together to break the ice. Off with your

boots and pants, but not the polypropylene longjohns and socks. You climb into the sled with Kanuti, wrestle into your sleeping bag, break open half a dozen hand warmers and close the sled bag over both of you.

Hours pass. You snack on jerky, chocolate, and seal oil, then drift fitfully in and out of sleep as your body warms next to Kanuti's. Your feet ache, but the frostbite looks light. Your broken arm swells and stiffens, and you tie it to your torso to minimize movement and further aggravation. The cabin is another twenty miles away. You must either get there yourself, or wait at least twenty-four hours for your buddies, who expect you no later than today. Twenty-four hours is too long. You pull on dry socks and pants and mukluks, then climb out of the sled and fire up the alcohol stove to heat snow for water. Nothing debilitates sled dogs more than dehydration. You take a long drink yourself, then pack up.

An hour later, you are back on the trail with Kanuti in lead harness. The dogs pull like horses, maintaining a steady trot. They have traveled this trail before and know there is a cabin not far ahead. Ten miles to go. Northern lights dance overhead, waving in yellows and greens. The trail is smooth, but the sled rides rough, probably damaged from the fall. Five miles to go: the home stretch. Like old friends, the winter constellations twinkle above, and a few minutes later, you round a bend and see the light you have been waiting for, a lamp burning outside a cabin. Crazy Creek.

Dogs bark, and your buddies step outside to meet you. You glide up and stop. Never have your buddies looked so good, or you so bad. Suddenly you feel weak, and one of them helps you inside while the others care for your dogs.

The fire is warm; the stew, steaming. A bowlful is placed in front of you, but something is wrong. You have a debt to pay. You climb to your feet, grab the stew, and hobble outside. Your dogs look up. They have just eaten but could eat some more, and on this winter night, each receives a ladleful of hot moose stew, with two helpings for Kanuti, the dog that comes along only once in a lifetime, if ever.

▶ *Englishman Roy Monk attends to his huskies' needs in Rohn after crossing Rainy Pass during the Iditarod Trail Sled Dog Race.*

◄ Pirate, an Alaskan husky belonging to musher Matt Desalernos, rests in Kaltag during the Iditarod Trail Sled Dog Race. From Kaltag, the race climbs over Old Woman Portage to Unalakleet, then follows the coast to Nome. ▲ In Rohn, Joe Redington, Sr., the "Father of the Iditarod," talks with Libby Riddles. In 1985, Riddles became the first woman to win the Iditarod. Her picture appeared in publications around the world, and interest in the Iditarod began to soar.

▲ Like many mushers, Kathy Hobgood wears her mittens on "idiot strings" around her back for quick access. ▶ At -20°F, a frosty-faced husky in Marc Poage's team arrives in Circle on the Yukon Quest International Sled Dog Race. ▶ ▶ Spectators cheer Gunnar Johnson into the Eagle River checkpoint, twenty miles north of Anchorage on the Iditarod Trail Sled Dog Race. From Eagle River, the teams are transported by truck to a restart of the race in Wasilla.

◄ Lavon Barve mushes his team over wind-sculpted ice and snow on frozen Norton Sound, near Elim and the end of the Iditarod Trail Sled Dog Race. ▲ Jennifer Wippich prepares for her first dogsled ride along the old Stampede Trail near Healy. ► ► Backdropped by peaks of the Alaska Range, Jeff King's team breaks trail on a training run near his home on Goose Lake. A champion musher, he trains his dogs year-round and studies their performance carefully.

▲ More than twenty veterinarians volunteer on the Iditarod each year, giving advice to mushers and medications to dogs. Here, John Ace (right) confers with veterinarian Bob Sept on the condition of the paws of his team dog, Tina. If the dog is too sore to continue, Sept and Ace will agree to "drop" her from the race.
► With a fast run behind them, huskies wait in the low light of a January afternoon to be unhooked and unharnessed at Tudor Track, in Anchorage.

CHAPTER FOUR

Strictly Speaking

The best long distance runners eat raw meat, run naked and sleep in the snow. Allow us to present the dogs of the world-famous Iditarod Trail Sled Dog Race. Not your average canine. If you want these guys to fetch the morning paper, plan on throwing it 1,049 miles . . . While most dogs can learn go fetch, these dogs have learned to fly.
> ALASKA AIRLINES, sponsor of the Iditarod Trail
> Veterinarian Program, and presenter of the Leonhard
> Seppala Award for humanitarian treatment of the dogs

I couldn't see the trail. Many times I couldn't even see my dogs, so blinding was the gale. I gave Balto, my lead dog, his head and trust to him. He never faltered. It was Balto who led the way. The credit is his.
> GUNNAR KAASEN, long-distance musher,
> on arriving in diphtheria-stricken Nome
> with life-saving serum, February 1925

I got my snow machine up to the top of Topkok Hills and got off and lay on my back in the snow to look at the northern lights all over the sky.
> TONY LAMM, trailbreaker

Here is a pleasure which you unfortunate outsiders can never even form an idea of: Dog driving! Our dogs are other animals, I can assure you, than the little rats you see in the civilized world; and a Newfoundland, though large, compares with them, from his clumsiness, as a hippopotamus would with a deer.
> ROBERT KENNICOTT, naturalist and Alaska explorer, 1866

I think the Iditarod is three things. It's a highly competitive sporting event, it's a business and needs to be run as such, and it's a celebration of the history and spirit of Alaska.
> JACK NIGGEMYER, former Iditarod race manager

◄ Two mushers ride tandem on a training run to evaluate their dogs as they glide into a sinking, January sun near Anchorage.

Unless you're the lead dog, the scenery never changes.
> BUMPER STICKER

Muscles, bones and lungs—these dogs are running machines.
> DR. BOB BJERK, Iditarod veterinarian

She was part of the family, like a kid. But I can't be bummed out. I'll cry some more after the race.
> MARTIN BUSER, long-distance musher, after Stafford,
> his lead dog, died on the Iditarod Trail at Rainy Pass

The worst thing you can do is ask a dog team—or a man for that matter—to do more than it's willing to do. That's what breaks their will . . . You have to treat your dogs so that they never lose their desire to go.
I like going around the corner on one runner of the sled.
I have two speeds: full tilt and off.
That one dog will either make you or break you. Races are won or lost by the dogs you leave in the truck.
A clean run starts with a clean truck.
> CHARLIE CHAMPAINE, short-distance musher

You've got to feed 'em good and treat 'em right.
> GARETH WRIGHT, short-distance musher

Challenge is the Iditarod's spine, and history is its soul, but love of dogs and mushing will always be its heart.
The Iditarod Race is a geographic odyssey of epic proportions. Mushers who reach the burled arch on Nome's Front Street may find their lives transformed but, as a symbol of frontier heritage, the race has greater value. Just watching it wakens the bold voyager slumbering deep within us all.
Thinking racers tinker with teams like auto racers tuning an engine, shifting dog positions for better performance. Even leaders are subject to change. Each animal is carefully evaluated, and the weary are dropped at the next checkpoint.
> TONY DAWSON, field editor, Alaska Magazine, and
> former Iditarod veterinarian

"We're ready when you are."

You started to get the feeling that the clock was ticking, that if the wind doesn't get you, the moisture will.
> BURT BOMHOFF, long-distance musher referring to when he and three others were pinned down on Norton Sound for 36 hours as 60-mph winds rocked their sleds and buried their dogs in snow

This is the most fun I've had with my clothes on in years.
> ANONYMOUS CELEBRANT, in a tavern in Nome at the end of the Iditarod Trail Sled Dog Race

If [Governor] Hickel can make a comeback, I can make a comeback.
The whole town is interested. It's like the main event of everything you do. It's like the Super Bowl.
> GEORGE ATTLA, short-distance musher and author

I live in those storms all winter long. I got a pretty good idea what they can do. I know a lot of people who died out there snowmachining. It happens all the time.
> JERRY AUSTIN, long-distance musher

You do everything. You are the nutritionist. You are the builder. You don't become good at it overnight.
> JANET CLARKE, short-distance musher

You watch guys who would never even think of changing a diaper out here babying dogs. It's kind of funny, actually.
> TOM DAILY, long-distance musher

Norman still drives the way they did in the '20s and '30s. He doesn't travel light. He's always got a come-along, and a brake that would stop the Gates of Hell from closing, and three sleeping bags, and so many watches strapped to his arm he looks like a thief from Brooklyn.
> SHELLEY GILL, long-distance musher, author, and publisher, speaking about Colonel Norman Vaughan, the oldest musher to race the Iditarod

We adhere to the make-the-most-out-of-what-you-have approach. We try to maximize each dog's potential.
> KATHY FROST, short-distance musher

When the dogs stop, they really stop. It's like having a flat tire.
> HOWARD LINCOLN, checker

I swear I kept thinking all those reports I heard on the radio were fake, that there was no race. I didn't see anybody else on the trail.
> DIANA DRONENBERG, long-distance musher

I didn't have the proper gear, and the cold just devastated me . . . I started shaking violently . . . Marine boot camp was more fun than this.
> JON GLEASON, long-distance musher speaking of the Yukon Quest at -60°F.

It's real sad at the end of the race [Iditarod]. You've got these people who have been on the trail to the bitter end, running freight sleds, and they haven't changed sleds, haven't had duPont to sponsor them. They're wearing Carhartt's and using duct tape to hold their mittens together, and they come down Front Street [in Nome] and there's six people to greet them.
> LANA HARRIS, race volunteer

It's scary being the last one on the trail.
> BOB HOYTE, long-distance musher who finished the Iditarod ten days behind the leaders

Well, give me a team with a good lead dog
   and a sled that's built so fine.
And let me race those miles to Nome,
   one thousand-forty-nine.
And when I get back to my home,
   hey, I can tell my tale.
I did, I did, I did
   the Iditarod Trail.
> HOBO JIM, singer, songwriter, and musician

Gareth Wright loads a husky after a race.

What I feel is, if I died right now, it'd be okay.
    LIBBY RIDDLES, long-distance musher and author,
    when she became the first woman to win
    the Iditarod, March 1985

I'm lucky to get three hours sleep for every twenty-four hours on the trail.

The dogs are athletes, and the musher is their coach. They work together as a team, and hopefully, the musher is never the weak link.

When the dogs are racing, 3 percent dehydration can mean 20 percent loss in performance.
    JEFF KING, long-distance musher

But, hey, what do I know? Before coming up here, the only thing I'd seen a dog pull was my socks—from one room to another.

I take these scenes from a week of the Iditarod; I see the craziness of the start in downtown Anchorage, where serious racers mix with dreamers. I see all those dogs, hundreds of them, their snouts covered by icicles and they trudge on. I see mushers in the woods, cooking meat, dipping into an ice hole for water. I see Joe Garnie, the ebullient Alaskan who won a Dodge truck for being the first to reach a certain checkpoint, telling me "This is great. Now I gotta get a driver's license." I see the solitary beauty of Finger Lake, the majesty of Rainy Pass. I see a line of dogs pulling a musher through white mountains as big as God's soldiers. I see myself cleaning off my boots after stepping in a pile of you-know-what.
    MITCH ALBOM, award-winning columnist for the
    Detroit Free Press, covering his first Iditarod

The cheapest and most important element in a dog's diet is water.
    DR. ROLAND LOMBARD, short-distance musher

There is no faith which has never yet been broken, except that of a truly faithful dog.
    DR. KONRAD Z. LORENZ, psychologist and author

Top drivers like Susan Butcher switch sleds more often than Elizabeth Taylor switches husbands.

Aside from winning, my only objective is to finish with ten fingers and ten toes.

I'll never forget looking up to see the sky ablaze with a rainbow of northern lights as we glided slowly up the Yukon River . . . or the picture of the sun setting across the frozen Bering Sea in an orange and purple haze as I stood in the wind at Shaktoolik.
    TIM MOWRY, long-distance musher
    and sports writer for the *Fairbanks Daily News Miner*

Why do I want to win? Because my dogs deserve to win.

They're tired. They didn't have a conference and go on strike. They gave me everything they had, then ran out of gas.

Little noises—whistles, calls, things like that—add up to a lot of stress. I only talk to my dogs when I need an extraordinary effort from them.

This sport has done wonderful things for Alaska. Dog care has improved by leaps and bounds, and people realize now that the better they treat their dogs, the better their dogs will perform.

To be successful in today's Iditarod you need a solid sponsor, or you need to be independently wealthy.
    DEE DEE JONROWE, long-distance musher

You pick up these articles about Alaska, talking all about how it's the last frontier and you're thinking to yourself, "Right. You just jump on the interstate to Nome, then take a left and go to Fairbanks." I had no idea until I came here that there were no roads to any of those places. What I wasn't prepared for was that there wasn't a road, a street light, an advertising sign or a building in sight.
    LYNN SWANN, professional football player-turned-
    commentator for ABC's "Wide World of Sports"

She ain't turning back and she ain't waiting for anybody.
    JOE GARNIE, long-distance musher speaking of
    Libby Riddles en route to her becoming
    the first woman to win the Iditarod, March 1985

A musher's credo on the bumper of his dog truck

We used to have this guy in our village, and he was kind of a wimp. Even his name was wimpy—Carroll. And one day, he said he wanted to try the Iditarod. We all laughed, figuring, how's this guy [going to] make it eleven hundred miles, right? But Carroll rented a dog team, and he trained them, and then the race came. And darn if he didn't fall and break his arm in the first stretch. We figured, that's it. But you know what? They flew him to a hospital, and he had the arm set and went back to the dogs. He finished the race, made it all the way to Nome. We couldn't believe it. It changed our opinion of him. He was different after that. That's the Iditarod, I guess. It changes people.

    JIM OKONEK, glacier pilot and owner of
    Talkeetna-based K₂ Aviation, as told to Mitch Albom,
    columnist, *Detroit Free Press*

Some people today want to make the Iditarod Race easier, and follow different routes than the original trail. I think that's wrong. The old-timers that built that trail through the woods didn't do it because they needed the exercise, they did it because they knew it was the best all-season route. It's important that the race honor the trail, and follow it.

    JOE REDINGTON, SR., long-distance musher and Father of
    the Iditarod Trail Sled Dog Race

A man driving a dog team is sometimes the biggest dog himself.
    HARRY KARSTENS, long-distance musher
    and first superintendent of
    Mt. McKinley [Denali] National Park, 1921-28

There was nothing for it but to face the music. The dogs did their best, and I drove as if we were in a race.
    LEONHARD SEPPALA, legendary long-distance musher,
    about carrying life-saving diphtheria serum to Nome in 1925

If the dogs really look good when you cross the finish line, that means you did everything right. That means they were really moving. That means you had maximum speed.
    JOE RUNYAN, long-distance musher

For Susan Butcher, happiness is not having to run out of the outhouse to answer the phone.
    SONJA STEPTOE, writer, *Sports Illustrated* magazine

It's not until you've won it that you realize how fickle a thing victory is . . . The variable is seventy-five other individuals all wanting the same thing—as bad or more than you do.
    RICK SWENSON, long-distance musher and author

How can you be discouraged when you are doing something you love?
    COLONEL NORMAN VAUGHAN, long-distance musher,
    explorer, and author

You will often find more dog manure in a mushing conversation than in any dog lot.
    JIM WELCH, short-distance musher and author of *The
    Speed Mushing Manual: How to Train Racing Sled Dogs*

She [Susan Butcher] probably has forty dogs in her lot that could make our team. We've probably got six that could make hers.
    DEAN OSMAR, long-distance musher

I had uncontrollable sleep attacks. Going into Ophir one night, there was a big full moon. It was 40 below. I hadn't slept since Nikolai. I was running with my headlamp off and listening to wild, spooky music on my tape deck. I was extremely tired. And then I began having feelings of anti-gravity. I felt if I let go of the handle-bars, I would just float up into the sky.

When you finally see the lights of Nome, you're psyched. It's over. You could sleep for three months. But as soon as you've slept and had enough to eat, you start wishing the trail went on forever.

    MACGILL ADAMS, long-distance musher and
    wilderness guide

▶ A musher glides beneath a bluff at sunset on the Yukon River, between Ruby and Galena on the Iditarod Trail Sled Dog Race.

◄ Departing Rohn, Laird Barron mushes down the frozen South Fork of the Kuskokwim River en route to the next checkpoint in Nikolai, more than ninety miles away. ▲ Robin Jacobsen drives his team along the north flank of the Alaska Range during the Iditarod Trail Sled Dog Race. ►► In Ruby, Linwood Fiedler's huskies rest on straw that has been flown into each Iditarod checkpoint by a team of volunteer pilots, popularly called the "Iditarod Air Force."

▲ Sunrise washes over the Yukon at -30°F as a musher slides upriver from
Anvik to Grayling on the southern route of the Iditarod Trail Sled Dog Race.
▶ John Barron mushes through muskeg, tundra, and spruce forest blanketed in
snow near Cripple Landing, the halfway point on the northern route of the
Iditarod.   ▶ ▶ Patty Rich waits to run her team during a January sunrise at
eleven o'clock and -25°F, at the Jeff Studdert Race Grounds in Fairbanks, Alaska.

◄ Smoke climbs above a cabin at Angel Creek, one of only nine checkpoints on the thousand-mile Yukon Quest. ▲ Iditarod champion Joe Runyan takes a few minutes at 2:00 A.M. to answer questions from media and townsfolk at Unalakleet. A perennial front-runner, he keeps pace with competitors by efficiently strawing, watering, feeding, and medicating his dogs. He will then get a bite to eat, maybe a nap, and be back on the trail to Nome in a few hours.

▲ Amid a light snowfall, musher Jerry Austin consults with veterinarians and checkers at midnight in Rohn about dropping one of his dogs that developed a limp crossing Rainy Pass. Because a team of ten strong dogs can travel faster than a team of twenty tired ones and dog care is of high priority, dropping dogs on the Iditarod Trail Sled Dog Race is common. ▶ Like most mushers, Jim and Nancy Nolke have a dog truck to haul their huskies from their home to a race.

◄ Tim Mowry's team rests in the late February sunshine in Circle during the Yukon Quest Sled Dog Race. Because overheating and dehydration can be a serious problem for dogs at midday, many mushers prefer to travel at night. ▲ A sprint team flies down Tudor Track on a training run during a January sunset in Anchorage. ► ► Recreational musher Jennifer Wolk drives her team along the old Stampede Trail on the north boundary of Denali National Park.

▲ With an arm raised to shield his eyes from the sun, a musher drives his team past frosted birches, spruce, and the Chugach Mountains near Anchorage. ▶ Alaskan huskies wait to be unharnessed after a speed race. The red on their necks is paint, put there the first day of the race to mark them and prohibit mushers from introducing fresh dogs into their teams. ▶ ▶ A musher and team head toward Finger Lake and the Alaska Range early in the Iditarod.

CHAPTER FIVE

The Dogs
of
Denali

It is summer in Denali National Park and Preserve, one of the most popular tourist destinations in Alaska. From dawn till dusk, May to September, tour buses and shuttle buses rumble along a single, winding dirt road through this six-million-acre subarctic sanctuary, carrying visitors who stare out the windows with great anticipation, watching for wildlife. They see Dall sheep, caribou, moose, wolves, red foxes, golden eagles, and grizzly bears. They see a vast, sweeping land lifting at its edges into the icy, crenulated battlements of the Alaska Range. They attend ranger-led discovery hikes, nature walks, and history talks. They laugh. They rest. They bow to see a saxifrage and lift their eyes to the massif called Mount McKinley, or Denali, rising head and shoulders above everything around it, the highest mountain in North America.

Summer, however, is not a complete picture of Alaska's premier national park, and the visitors know it. They know there is a longer, colder, darker side with northern lights and frozen nights.

And they wonder, what is it like here in winter?

It is no surprise, then, that among their summer experiences in Denali, one of the most memorable for visitors is the ever-popular sled dog demonstration, otherwise known as "the doggie-demo." This is an hour-long window into winter and the park's history that is held three times a day, from May to September, at the dog kennels behind headquarters.

The buses arrive. The visitors file out and walk down a gravel path where a park ranger greets them in a handsome, class-A, green and gray uniform beneath a broad-brimmed beaver felt hat.

"Welcome," she says. "Go ahead and walk around to meet the dogs if you'd like. The demonstration will begin in a few moments."

Settled among the spruce are two long rows of wooden dog houses, each with a post and swivel in front, and a husky chained to it. The dogs greet the visitors with mixed reactions, just as the visitors greet them. Some are outgoing; some are shy. Some are loud; some are quiet. Those dogs in heat, with medical problems, or too rambunctious for small children, are kept in cages.

All in all, however, the two dozen huskies in the Denali Park Kennels are among the most approachable sled dogs in Alaska, bred not just for a willingness to work, but for friendliness as well. They meet more than thirty thousand visitors each summer and hold an honored role in the tradition of winter patrols in the park.

A sign above the entrance of each house gives the name of the dog. From the candy litter comes Lic'rice, Taffy, Gumdrop, Roca, and Fudge; from the star litter, Gemini, Orion, and Cassi; from the weather litter, Typhoon, Tempest, and Gale; from the Celtic litter, Druid, Mystic, and Merlin; and from the Berry litter (named by park superintendent Russell Berry), Blue, Bear, and Cloud.

In five minutes, the crowd is charmed—and the program has not even begun. Senior citizens photograph each other with the dogs. Children find their favorites and pet them. And a few people gather at the dog house nearest the main building to admire the most special Denali husky of them all: Mitts, the kennel matriarch.

Eleven years old and retired, she lies atop her dog house with her front paws crossed, her tail wagging, her ears down, her eyes blue and calm.

"Native legend says that blue-eyed dogs can see the wind," the ranger tells the people admiring Mitts.

"Can they really?" a small boy asks.

"Well," the ranger says as she kneels next to him, "It's hard to say. We can see the wind in some ways, how it bends trees and moves leaves along the ground. Maybe Mitts can see the wind in other ways. Ways we don't understand. Sled dogs have been in Alaska with Eskimos and Athabascans for thousands of years. Maybe they know something we don't."

The boy looks at Mitts. "Is it true, Mitts? Can you really see the wind?" Mitts wags her tail.

Smiling, the ranger steps away, plugs in her portable microphone, motions to the crowd, and says, "If everyone will gather here in a large circle, we'll begin the program."

Eighty people from New York to New Mexico circle around as the ranger says, "You've probably figured out by now that I'm not Sergeant Preston, and there's no Yukon King here. But sled dogs have been a tradition in this park since it was created seventy-five years ago. I'd like to share a slice of that tradition with you. . . ."

◀ *A musher's-eye view looks beyond a dog team, up a trail to the Alaska Range on a clear, March evening in Denali National Park.*

Mitts, matriarch of the Denali Kennels

For twenty minutes she regales the crowd with facts and stories from the old days. "Sled dogs used to be the only means of travel through this park," she tells them. "In fact, Harry Karstens, the park's first superintendent, was hired in 1921 because of his knowledge of the area and his ability to drive sled dogs. He was headquartered in Nenana, with his primary duty to protect the park's wildlife from illegal hunting and trapping.

"Each new ranger hired back then was assigned a team of seven dogs and a district of the park to patrol. They mushed three to four hundred miles each month, erected tents and built cabins, marked the park boundaries, and visited outlying settlements to inform the residents about the park and its regulations. By 1936, the park's kennels had fifty dogs, and in 1939, these demonstrations began.

"We still run sled dog patrols here. In fact, of the fifty national parks in the United States and its territories, only Denali can claim a continuous history of dogsledding. The patrols are important to census wildlife, monitor aircraft, and stock cabins. And they are great fun. . . ." Her voice trails off.

The crowd is quiet; the dogs are still. A gray jay flies by. A red squirrel chatters. The ranger looks around as someone asks, "Is this your favorite park?"

"Yes," she says. "I have worked as a river ranger in the Grand Canyon and a naturalist in the Everglades, but the most memorable season was the winter I spent here mushing dogs. There is nothing like it. Never have I worked so hard as I did on that first sled dog trip, hauling water, chopping wood, harnessing dogs, lifting sleds, tying lines, fixing meals, rising early, quitting late. There wasn't a feminine bone left in my body. But never will I forget the grand scenery and the silence. And the dogs that needed me as much as I needed them."

The crowd stirs; the dogs sit up.

"Please," the ranger says. "Nobody move until I tell you to. The dogs know the demonstration is about to begin. Five of them are going to get to run, and once we move, they will get excited and bark, and I will lose voice contact with you. So, here's what I want you to do. . . ."

The ranger gives precise instructions to the crowd about when to move, and where. "Ready?" she says. "Now."

The crowd moves into a straight line along the kennels' main building, and two dozen huskies jump to their feet and bark wildly. The ranger chooses the five lucky dogs and escorts them to the sled by lifting their forelegs off the ground, giving her the balance of power. Lic'rice will lead. Blue, Druid, Fudge, and Merlin will follow. Each is harnessed, barking, howling, and jumping. The crowd aims cameras and videocassette recorders. The sled has been outfitted with wheels and is anchored to a wooden post sunk deep in the ground. The ranger steps on the runners, secures her hat, reaches down, unhooks the sled, and is gone.

The dogs bolt down a gravel path and accelerate through the spruce forest to fifteen miles per hour. They bank sharply to the right and circle back toward the kennels with tongues out and feet flying. They are headed home, when suddenly a snowshoe hare hops across the path and into the woods.

Lic'rice turns in pursuit.

"No!" the ranger yells.

The team crashes through the forest; the hare escapes. People crane their necks to see what is happening. The kennel dogs bark wildly. Even Mitts is on her feet. It takes the ranger five minutes to untangle her team and get them back to where they began.

She stops the sled in front of the crowd, catches her breath, and says sheepishly, "Well, that doesn't happen very often."

The people are full of questions, and she answers them. They talk about their dogs back home, a favorite terrier, retriever, or mutt. They stand on the runners of the sled and take photographs of each other.

Time flies. The bus driver starts the engine. The crowd drifts away. Another Denali Sled Dog Demonstration is over. The ranger returns the five dogs to their houses, stores the equipment, and leaves. And soon the kennels are quiet.

But Mitts is on her feet again, staring into the forest. Is it a snowshoe hare she sees? A red squirrel? A gray jay?

Or is it the wind?

► *The Fur Rendezvous World Championship, run in Anchorage since 1946, attracts thousands to Alaska's largest city each February.*

◄ Cheryl Payne handles a pair of Alaskan huskies about to race for her friend and fellow musher, Carolyn McCormick, in Anchorage. Typical of Alaskan huskies—not a recognized pure breed—the dogs are random in appearance, smooth in temperament, and fleet of foot. For the next thirty minutes, these will run more than twenty mph and pull McCormick to a race victory. ▲ A team breaks into a clearing on Tudor Track, near Campbell Airstrip Road, Anchorage.

▲ Huskies belonging to François Varigas wait to be loaded onto an Alaska Airlines flight from Kotzebue to Anchorage. Transporting, feeding, and providing medical needs for sled dogs adds up to tens of thousands of dollars each year for a serious musher with a large kennel. To defray these costs, mushers recruit donations from sponsors.   ▶ Backdropped by the Chugach Mountains, Lorraine Temple takes her team on a training run in Moose Meadow, Girdwood.

◄ Arnold Woodward's team dashes for the finish in a seven-dog-class race on the Tudor Track in Anchorage. If the dogs cross the line with their tails wagging, they probably could have been pushed harder. If they are not on their feet an hour after the race, they were probably pushed too hard. Good mushers always place the welfare of their dogs above their finishing times. ▲ Alaskan huskies streak by at eighteen mph during the Fur Rendezvous World Championship.

▲ The amber light of sunrise spills across the frozen Yukon River and musher Jacques Philip as he drives his team through the lonely dawn toward Grayling, on the southern route of the Iditarod Trail. It is not unusual for mushers to fall asleep while traveling on their sleds, especially at night since good lead dogs can follow most trails in most conditions. ▶ Alaskan huskies Brownie and Toolick wait to run in the Orville Lake Memorial Sled Dog Race in Anchorage.

◄ On the road less traveled, Jeff King trains his team on the snowy lane leading to his home near Denali National Park.   ▲ Alaskan husky sprint dogs fly along Tudor Track at nearly twenty mph during the Anchorage Fur Rendezvous World Championship. Weighing about forty pounds, they have a smooth lope on tough feet; deep, narrow chests; long legs; and a flexible back for good extension. Three to seven years is the optimum age for performance in sprint dogs.

▲ The warmth of a midnight fire and friendly conversation makes waiting for the next musher easier at the Rohn checkpoint, on the Iditarod Trail. Seated left to right are veterinarian/musher Tom Cooley, checker Pat Plunkett, trapper Denny Weber, and race judge Dan Boyette. Without hundreds of volunteers, the Iditarod and other races could not exist.   ▶ ABC's "Wide World of Sports" interviews Rick Swenson shortly after he wins the Iditarod at 1:30 A.M. in Nome.

IDITAROD TRAIL
ALASKA

The Last Great Race 1049 mi Anchorage to Nome

IDITAROD TRAIL '91
RACE

Young
SIGNS

Dodge
Truck

Timberland

STEPHAN
FINE ARTS

FINISH

IAMS
PET FOODS

ALASCOM
ALASKA AIRLINES
National Bank of Alaska

1049

MILES

END OF IDITAROD DOG RA...

ANCHORAGE

◄ A team of Alaskan huskies wears the many eager faces of anticipation as they wait in a cart on the frozen Kotzebue Sound for the beginning of the Kobuk 440 Sled Dog Race. Barking and howling with excitement, they will fall silent once they hit the trail, with all their energy invested in a steady trot and firm pulling. ▲ A sunset in early April silhouettes recreational musher Jennifer Wolk and her sled dog team on the old Stampede Trail near Healy.

▲ A record snowfall nearly obscures a musher and dog team gliding through a January sunrise at the Jeff Studdert Race Grounds in Fairbanks. The musher is kicking—called pedaling—to increase speed. It is important that he not kick too hard and jerk the sled. This could break the dogs' smooth gait and even injure them.   ▶ Janet Clarke's wheel dogs, Mighty Mouse and Miss Mouse, look alert and ready to run again—a good sign—after racing twelve miles in Anchorage.

CHAPTER SIX

Susan Butcher's Dog-gone Dynasty

Rick Swenson and Jeff King, two of the world's best long-distance sled dog mushers, are in Ambler, Alaska, sharing defeat. Swenson kneels in the snow to replace the plastic runners on his overturned sled. He has done it so many times, it looks as though he could do it blindfolded. He rolls up the old runners—damaged on the rough trail from Shungnak—and tapes them together. King stands next to him, scratching his head. Their tired dogs are strawed and fed and bedded down. It will be hours before they hit the trail again.

Forty feet away another sled dog team is up and ready to leave—eager to leave, in fact. The team has traveled 240 miles and has another 200 to go. The villagers gather around—men, women, elders, children—for it is not every day that a sled dog race comes to town; and every onlooker, even Swenson and King, watches the fluid, calculated movements of Susan Butcher. She packs her sled. Her dogs have been watered, fed, and medicated; their paws, salved and bootied. It is time to go, and they are on their feet, barking with excitement.

King stares at them.

"They're just dogs," Swenson tells him.

"I know," King says, "but look at them. They act like they're just starting this race. I don't get it."

Swenson shrugs. "Just dogs, Jeff."

"Yeah," King says, "but these are not even her *best* dogs. She ran those in the Iditarod. She sold me one of her other dogs—one of her *expendable* dogs—and now it's one of the best in my kennel. How does she do it?"

Swenson shrugs.

King scratches his head.

The villagers step away. "Let's go," Butcher commands, and she's off. Her huskies pull firmly down to the frozen Kobuk River, bound for Kotzebue and another race victory, this time the Kobuk 440.

"My goal was never to be the first woman or the best woman to win the Iditarod," Susan Butcher once said. "It was to be the best dogsled racer." Period.

◄ *Victory-bound Susan Butcher glides past the Copper River and Mount Drum, in the Wrangell Mountains, in the Copper Basin 300.*

Joe Redington, Sr., father of the famous Iditarod Trail Sled Dog Race from Anchorage to Nome, remembers a young Susan Butcher who, years ago, apprenticed herself to him to learn the skill she has since mastered. "One morning when we were camping out," Redington said, "I saw her out barefoot in the snow with the droopiest drawers I'd ever seen. She was out there chopping wood. I got out of my sleeping bag and said, 'Where'd you get those drawers?' And she said, 'They're my dad's.'"

"I knew right then," Redington said, "that she had it."

The right stuff? Mind over matter? Alchemy? Whatever it is that perennial Iditarod champion Susan Butcher has, it works. Her dogs are the ones to watch. She is the musher to beat. In 1991, *Sports Illustrated* said, "This symbiotic relationship between Butcher and her dogs is the biggest reason why, at the age of thirty-six, she is considered the finest long-distance sled dog racer ever, and one of the greatest mushers of all time."

When in New York City to receive the award from the Women's Sports Foundation as the Professional Sportswoman of the Year, Butcher spoke about her Trail Breaker Kennels. She lives at the end of the road in Eureka, Alaska, with her husband, Dave Monson—also a champion musher—along with three assistants and 140 sled dogs.

"I know every dog's parents," she told the attentive audience. "I know every dog's grandparents. I know which one has a cold and which one didn't eat well last night, and I know each one's personality and where he likes to be scratched. You have to understand, this is all I care about, and this is all I think about. I don't understand anything else, and I don't care about anything else. I'm with my dogs twelve or sixteen hours a day, seven days a week. They're my friends and my family and my livelihood."

The bonding begins at the moment of birth, when the newborn puppies are lifted from their mother into Butcher's cradled arms. Hers is the first human scent they smell, the first voice they hear, the first face they see. It is a smiling face. From then on, she is their best friend.

She rises at six A.M. and opens her cabin door. "Good morning," she says through the brisk air, and more than one hundred dogs send up a chorus of howls. "Those dogs believe they can do

The town of Ruby welcomes Susan Butcher.

anything because Susan believes they can," said Butcher's friend, Dee Dee Jonrowe, herself a champion long-distance musher.

"I want the dogs to see me doing everything for them," Butcher says. "They have to trust me and know that I care about them and that I won't ask them to do something they aren't capable of." In her own magical way—through love, friendship, breeding, discipline, and a sixth sense—Butcher instills within her dogs two immutable desires: to be with humans, especially her, and to run in long-distance races, especially the Iditarod.

She feeds them, waters them, plays with them. A former veterinary technician and midwife to musk-oxen, she draws the dogs' blood, takes urine samples, gives physicals, and administers vaccinations. She recognizes the symptoms of maladies such as the often-fatal canine parvo virus, first diagnosed in 1978, and acute tracheobronchitis, called kennel cough, a contagious respiratory infection often characterized by a harsh, dry cough. Many times, she has stayed up all night with a sick dog, nursing it back to health, speaking in the same, reassuring voice that the dog heard at birth. It is one more ingredient in the recipe that makes her a champion.

None of this comes as any surprise to Susan's parents, Charlie and Agnes Butcher of Cambridge, Massachusetts. "She was always a very determined child," says Charlie. "There wasn't much chance of Susan's being pushed around." Or of Charlie raising her and her older sister, Kate, in a traditional manner, for he and Agnes did not subscribe to society's shallow limitations that dictated a "woman's place." He taught his girls to sail and build boats and bought them each a set of carpentry tools before they were teenagers. When they traveled to their summer home in Maine, Susan took to the wild country like a lead dog to the trail.

At age eight, after winning a school contest with her essay, "I Hate the City," she suggested that her parents tear down their home and build a log cabin to make more room for the things she loved. Wild things. Mountains. Forests. Wilderness. Go west, young woman.

Ten years later, in 1973, she was working as a boat builder and veterinary assistant in Boulder, Colorado, when she happened to pick up a copy of *Team & Trail* magazine with a story about the inaugural running of a race called the Iditarod. That was it. She packed her bags and moved to Alaska.

Soon she was chopping wood and mushing a small dog team at forty below zero in the wintry Wrangell Mountains and spending summers on a musk-ox farm in Fairbanks. In 1977, she met sixty-year-old Joe Redington, Sr., the legendary musher who owned one of the largest and strongest dog kennels in Alaska, and they made a deal: Butcher would help train Redington's younger dogs at his kennel in Knik, and he would loan her a few veteran huskies to enhance her breeding program and complete her team. It worked. In 1978, she entered the Iditarod for the first time and finished a respectable nineteenth.

Victory that year was one of the most memorable in Iditarod history, as Dick Mackey and Rick Swenson battled toward Nome together and ended up running down Front Street with their teams side by side. The crowd went wild. Mackey's lead dogs crossed the line first, but Swenson himself crossed before Mackey. Who won? "Make your decision and stick with it," Swenson told race officials as they discussed the problem. Finally, Dick Mackey was declared the winner by an incredible one second. It was a hard race to lose.

But the tables turned in 1982 when Rick Swenson won his fourth Iditarod (after victories in 1977, 1979, and 1981) by a narrow margin of only three minutes and forty-three seconds. The musher behind him? Susan Butcher. Every year, the woman with the brown ponytail had moved up in the placings, and people had begun to ask, could a woman win the Iditarod?

When Mary Shields and Lolly Medley became the first women to enter the race, in 1974, people doubted they could even finish. "You better turn around now; you'll never make it to Nome," yelled a man, as Shields drove her team out of Anchorage's Mulcahy Stadium. "I think that gave me great motivation, great encouragement to go on," she said. In the Athabascan village of Nulato, 760 miles into the race, her motivation strengthened. "I learned men were betting on which checkpoint the women would drop out at, and every time we left [a checkpoint], there were women raking in money," she said. "Those women were on my sled, too. I had to keep going for them." Keep going she did, finishing in

Iditarod Trail Committee headquarters in Wasilla

twenty-third place, one spot ahead of Medley. Eighteen men failed to finish that year.

Shields was not interested in making her mark for feminism or history; she just wanted to do what she loves: take a long mushing trip with her huskies. Not so Susan Butcher. She wanted to win; she still does. In the memorable words of Vince Lombardi, "Winning isn't everything, it's the only thing."

Early in the race of 1985, Butcher was in the lead and looking strong, when her team came over a blind hill and ran into an angry, pregnant moose in the middle of the trail. The dogs barked, the moose attacked, and for twenty minutes Butcher lived a nightmare, trying to hold off the moose with an axe. Then musher Duane Halverson arrived and killed the moose with his .44-caliber revolver. Butcher assessed the damage: two dogs dead, seven with head injuries, four with internal injuries, herself with a shoulder injury.

For Butcher, the 1985 Iditarod was over. Granite, her best leader, had tried to protect the team by attacking the moose's hindquarters and had been kicked and thrown against a tree. He lived, and a month later was back in harness for Butcher in the 350-mile-long Coldfoot Classic Sled Dog Race through Gates of the Arctic National Park.

The victory for the Iditarod that year went to Libby Riddles, the twenty-eight-year-old woman from Teller who had hunkered down in Shaktoolik with other front-runners to wait out a storm. Later, she had slipped away in the night to brave the blizzard and emerge alone on Front Street in Nome.

Not only had a woman won the Iditarod, but she had done it with absolute daring. Her blond hair, blue eyes, and smile appeared in newspapers everywhere, and the world sat up and took notice.

Had Riddles stolen Butcher's thunder? Yes. But Butcher's time was coming. Beginning in 1986, she won the Iditarod three times straight and shaved forty hours off the record for the race. In lead harness every time was Granite. "A Rambo-kind of dog," Swenson called the mild-mannered, dark-faced Granite, and then added, "When she loses that dog, she'll realize she's not as good as she thinks she is."

Granite aged. But then Tempy, Tolstoi, and Mattie took charge, filling the lead harness and showing incredible depth in Butcher's Trail Breaker Kennel as she continued to win races: the Iditarod, the Kuskokwim 300, the John Beargrease, the Kobuk 440, the Copper Basin 300, and the Arctic Coast 250.

How?

Parenting. "It eventually dawned on her that there are two, diametrically opposed views regarding sled dog excellence," wrote George Bryson in *We Alaskans* magazine. "It was the old debate between nature and nurture. One side . . . held that great leaders are primarily born, that a musher should be grateful if he's privileged to experience even one in his lifetime. For Swenson, that dog was Andy.

"But the other side (Butcher's) maintains that great leaders are primarily made, and that a dog with second-rate genes and first-rate training will always outperform a dog with first-rate genes and second-rate training."

Says Butcher, "When you've got a pup with the right breeding, the right genetics, you're just an eighth of the way there. It's not just that [other kennels] don't have good sperm and egg. That's not their problem. It's what they're doing with it after it hits the ground. That's the main thing—it's just work. It isn't magic. It's just work and work and work and work and work."

Call it a labor of love. Dog sledding has given Susan Butcher a field of dreams, and she has given dogsledding a renaissance. More young girls in schools across Alaska, when asked who they admire most, answer Susan Butcher.

When a thousand people gathered in Eagle River at the first checkpoint on the Iditarod Trail Sled Dog Race, half of them left after Susan Butcher went by. And when *We Alaskans* magazine did a feature story about her team, it bluntly called them, "the best dogs in the world."

Her dynasty will end; they all do. But her influence and contributions to the world of dogsledding will last a very long time, and descendants of her dogs—Ivak, Ali, Tekla, Granite, Tempy, Tolstoi, Mattie, Ruff, Spoons, Doc, Elan, Lightning—will run like the wind through the wilds of Alaska, winning races along with the hearts of spectators. What finer legacy could a musher ask for?

Jerky
Alaska Airlines
IAMS PET FOODS
National Bank of Alaska
ALASCOM
IDITAROD
CHAMPION
1990
Timberland
MILES
OG RACE
OME
Timberland
69

◄ Susan Butcher claims her fourth Iditarod victory in Nome in 1990. Kneeling to her side is bearded Leo Rasmussen, former mayor of Nome and eternal promoter of the Iditarod spirit. ▲ Stone and Galloway, second-string Alaskan huskies in Susan Butcher's Trail Breaker Kennels, rest in Ambler during the Kobuk 440 Sled Dog Race. ► ► Mushers and their teams rest at the Skwentna checkpoint, on the frozen Skwentna River, on the second day of the Iditarod.

◄ Klondike, a wheel dog belonging to Jacques Philip, rests on straw during the Kobuk 440. The booties, usually removed when a dog is not running, protect the dog's paws from rough ice, rock, and snow. ▲ Hang on! A novice musher fights to stay on the sled as his team flies down Fairbanks' Second Avenue during a businessmen's fun race. ▶ ▶ Dee Dee Jonrowe, a perennial top finisher in the Iditarod, mushes down the Yukon River at daybreak near Ruby.

▲ Villagers in Ambler gather to watch champion musher Susan Butcher straw her dogs after arriving from Kiana, down the Kobuk River. Not until she has fully tended to her dogs' needs will she tend to her own, a signature of her success.

▶ Stubby, a malamute on Catherine Mormile's team, rests in Rohn during the Iditarod. Malamutes are generally larger and slower than Alaskan huskies.

▶▶ Dave Dalton heads into a February sunset near Circle, on the Yukon Quest.

CHAPTER SEVEN

A Musher's Glossary

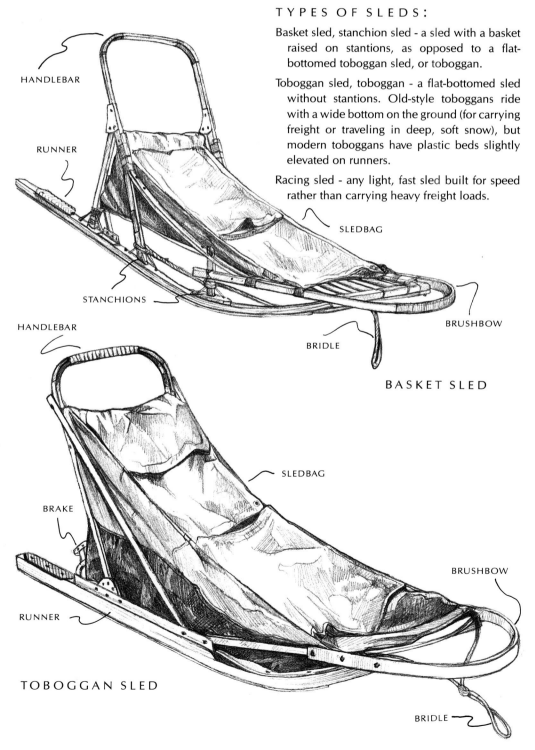

TYPES OF SLEDS:

Basket sled, stanchion sled - a sled with a basket raised on stantions, as opposed to a flat-bottomed toboggan sled, or toboggan.

Toboggan sled, toboggan - a flat-bottomed sled without stantions. Old-style toboggans ride with a wide bottom on the ground (for carrying freight or traveling in deep, soft snow), but modern toboggans have plastic beds slightly elevated on runners.

Racing sled - any light, fast sled built for speed rather than carrying heavy freight loads.

PARTS OF THE SLED:

Basket - the part of a dogsled where a musher stores gear.

Brake - any device, usually with a metal tooth or claw, attached to the rear of a dogsled and upon which the musher stands to slow or stop the sled.

Bridle - the loop of rope or cable that joins the gangline (and the pulling power of the dogs) to the front of the sled.

Brush bow - a strong piece of wood, metal, or plastic that curves forward from the front of a dogsled and acts as a fender to prevent sudden stops and breakage.

Handlebar - the arched rail at the back of a dogsled which is grasped by a musher while riding or pedaling.

Runners - the two long bottom pieces of the sled that extend behind the basket where the musher stands. Also, the replaceable strips of plastic or steel that make contact with snow and ice. If trail conditions change, mushers will often change their runners.

Sled bag - a cloth covering that fits in a dogsled's basket and contains the load. Closed on top by buckles, velcro, and/or a zipper.

Snow hook, brush hook, hook - a heavy, metal device with curved prongs attached to the bridle. Used to anchor the team at stops. Can be hooked around a tree, kicked into the snow, or pounded into the ice.

Stanchion - an upright support in the frame of a basket sled.

EQUIPMENT:

Booties - small dog socks made of denim, polar fleece, trigger cloth, etc., and often brightly colored and strapped with velcro, used to protect the dogs' feet from rough snow, ice, and rock. Required on all long-distance races.

HANDLEBAR

RUNNER

STANCHIONS

SLEDBAG

BRUSHBOW

BRIDLE

BASKET SLED

HANDLEBAR

BRAKE

RUNNER

SLEDBAG

BRUSHBOW

TOBOGGAN SLED

BRIDLE

Dog box - the compartment for dogs built onto the back of a dog truck.

Dog truck - any truck, van, or other vehicle (sometimes a bus) modified to carry a dog team and its gear.

Headlamp - a bright, battery-powered light that is worn on the musher's forehead to illuminate the dogs and trail at night. The battery pack rests on the belt or on the strap of the headlamp itself.

Harness - a nylon webbing device that comfortably fits a sled dog over its shoulders and along its back, thus transferring the dog's pulling power into the lines and back to the sled.

Jingler - a noisemaker used by mushers to make dogs run faster (though not all mushers think they are a good idea).

Mail pouch - a packet of letters or mementos (caches, postcards, etc.) carried by each team on long races—sometimes as required gear—then sold as souvenirs by race organizations.

Mukluks - Native-style winter footwear made of moosehide or sealskin with a canvas top, and thickly insulated with wool.

Toggle - a short piece of carved ivory or wood originally used by Eskimos to slip through a loop in the tugline for connection to a dog's harness. Snaps also can be used.

LINES:

Gangline - the main line that transfers the pulling power from the tuglines back to the sled.

Neckline - the short, usually slack line that joins the dog's collar to the gangline; taut only when a dog is pulling far to one side.

Picket line, stake-out line - a long chain, cable, or rope to which dogs are tethered during extended rests, or when camping.

Snubline - a stout rope that connects to the dog team via the bridle (like the snow hook) and serves to anchor the team to posts or trees before starting a run.

Tugline, tug, backline - the length of rope that joins a dog's harness to the gangline. Mushers study each dog's tugline to determine how hard it is pulling.

COMMANDS:

"Hike!" "Mush!" "All right!" "Let's go!" - commands for a dog team to get going ("Mush" probably comes from the French word "Marche," meaning walk, a command used by early French mushers and mutated over time into "mush.")

"Gee!" - turn to the right.

"Haw!" - turn to the left.

"Come gee!" "Come haw!" - turn 180 degrees in either direction.

"Get up!" - pull harder, pick up speed.

"On-by!" - keep going (past an obstacle or a distraction).

"Trail!" - from one musher to another, requesting right-of-way on the trail (for passing).

"Line out!" - commanding the lead dog to pull the team out straight from the sled, enabling the musher to hook or unhook the team.

"Whoa!" - slow down, stop (often accompanied with pressure on the brake).

IN MOTION:

Lope - a fast run with a long, easy stride typical of sprint dogs in short-distance races.

Pedaling, pumping, kicking - the one-legged push mushers use to help move the sled.

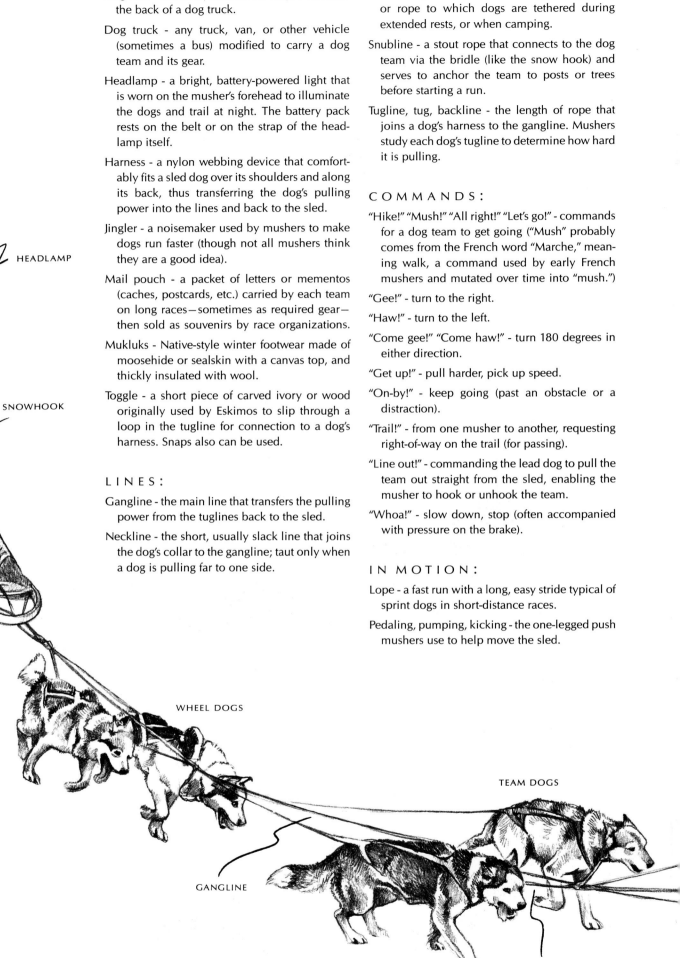

HEADLAMP

SNOWHOOK

WHEEL DOGS

GANGLINE

TEAM DOGS

NECKLINE

Trot - the prevalent gait of long-distance sled dogs that, with good trail conditions, can maintain a 10 to 12 mph trot for hours. A smooth, fluid movement, with diagonally opposite legs moving together, front left with rear right, and front right with rear left.

DOGS:

Husky - a loose term for a northern type of dog.

Alaskan husky - a small mixed breed that is native to the Athabascan villages of Interior Alaska. Not a pure breed, but regarded today as the best sled dog in the world. Average weight: 35-55 pounds. Average height: 21-23 inches at the shoulder.

Aurora husky - a type of Alaskan husky characterized by red hair, blue eyes, floppy ears, and tremendous speed, developed by musher Gareth Wright when he crossed Siberian huskies, wolves, and Irish setters.

Siberian husky - a pure breed native to Russia and distinguished by blue eyes (but not always), a handsome facial mask, and a thick coat. Used by early mushers, but since found to have less durability and a weaker trail appetite than the Alaskan husky. Average weight: 40-60 pounds. Average height: 21-23 inches at the shoulder.

Malamute - a pure breed, thick-coated husky favored by Klondike miners and early mushers for hauling heavy loads. Too large and too slow for modern sled dog racing. Average weight: 70-90 pounds. Average height: 25 inches at the shoulder.

Samoyed - a pure breed of white husky (named for a tribe of Native people in Siberia) with hair too long and endurance too poor for modern sled dog racing.

Hound - non-northern dogs—greyhound, saluki, coon hound, etc.—not commonly regarded as sled dogs, but regularly bred into the racing huskies.

Leader(s), lead dog(s) - the dog(s) that run in front position and thus determine the team's direction of travel.

Command leader - a lead dog capable of following voice commands to steer a team along an exact heading.

Swing dog(s), point dog(s) - the dog(s) in harness directly behind the lead dog(s).

Wheel dog(s), wheeler(s) - the dog(s) closest to the sled at the rear of the team. Often the largest and strongest dog(s) on the team.

Team dog(s) - any dog(s) on a team other than the lead, swing, and wheel dogs.

Dropped dog - a dog too tired, sick, or injured to continue, is "dropped" at a checkpoint, cared for by race personnel, and returned to the musher after the race.

RACE LENGTHS:

Long-distance - run continuously 300 miles or more (usually through wilderness).

Mid-distance - run continuously 100 to 300 miles (usually through wilderness).

Speed race, sprint race (short-distance) - daily runs of usually three to thirty miles run over the same trail in heats of one, two, or three days, totaling less than 100 miles (and usually run in and around villages, towns, and cities).

ALONG THE TRAIL:

Attitude - a positive frame of mind, and the desire to run and pull, essential in a good sled dog.

Broken/unbroken trail - "breaking" trail in the winter means making the first passage through fresh snow. The same trail is often repeatedly "broken" during winter (after each storm).

Checker - the race official who oversees arrival and departure of teams from a checkpoint.

Checkpoint - a designated site along a race trail—sometimes a village, or merely a solitary cabin or even a tent in the wilderness—where teams sign in and out, and often rest, resupply, and receive dog care and veterinary checks.

Food drop - the supply and resupply of food and provisions—usually by small plane—for dogs and mushers at checkpoints on long-distance wilderness races.

Handler - an assistant who helps a musher in the handling and training of dogs before and sometimes during a race.

Mandatory gear - various items a musher is required to carry in the sled on a long-distance race—usually a sleeping bag, snowshoes, an axe, dog booties, a headlamp, and a race promotion packet.

Mandatory layover - a required rest that each team must take during a race, usually a specific number of hours at a designated checkpoint.

Musher, driver - someone driving a team of dogs.

Overflow - water, saturated snow, or slush caused by a lake or river flooding up and over existing surface ice.

Portage - any trail used in summer or winter to connect two bodies of water.

Pressure ridge - a wall of ice created by the movement, expansion, and collision of ice on a river, a lake, or the sea.

Race marshall, chief judge - the final authority on rules and decisions at a sled dog race.

Skidoo, snow machine - slang for a snowmobile.

Sponsor - an individual, company, or institution that provides material and/or finances to help support a racing team, or the race in general.

Vet - a veterinarian (at least one veteranian is required at every checkpoint on most major long-distance races).

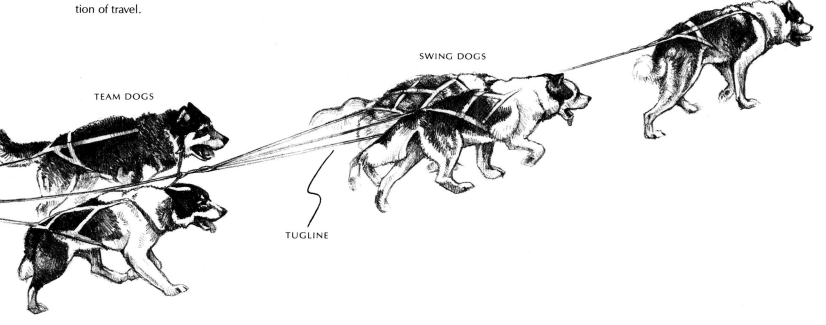

LEAD DOG

SWING DOGS

TEAM DOGS

TUGLINE

ACKNOWLEDGMENTS

Teamwork
on the
Trail

Just as dogsledding is a team effort, so was the creation of this book. Special appreciation goes to the Iditarod Trail Committee for logistical support on the Last Great Race.

And to those who shared their knowledge, excitement, friendship, hospitality, and their love of dogs and Alaska—a sincere thanks to you all:

Alaska Airlines
Alaska Magazine
Anchorage Daily News
Larry Anderson
John Auliye
Tom Bailey
Baker Aviation
Lori Baker
Ray Bane
John Barron
Bill and Peggy Bear
Greg Bill
Robert Bjerk
Bonnie Bless-Boenish
Hans Boenish
Weymouth Bowles
Dan Boyette
Dave Breuer
Larry, Karla, Leah, and Becky Bright
Chris Brown
Dave Brown
Jim Brown
George Bryson
Stan, Gretchen, and Erin Carrick
Craig Coggins
Chris Converse
Tom Cooley
Roy Corral
Pat Danly
Kathy and Tony Dawson
Jeannette DeMallie
Detroit Free Press
Joe and Rita Dold
Fairbanks Daily News Miner
Mark Farrington
Carol Foster
Jim and Connie Frerichs
Frank Ganley
Donna Gates-King
Patricia Gochenaur
Dominique Grandjean
Al Grillo
Bill Hall
Charles B. Hall
Melanie Heacox

Kelly Heck
Fred Hirschmann
Kathy Hobgood
Hobo Jim Music Company ASCAP
Iditarod Air Force
Clifford Jerue
William Johnson
Dee Dee Jonrowe
Cali and Tessa King
Jeff King
Sandy Kogl
Gary Koy
Jim Lavrakas
Bobby Lee
Bruce Lee
Al Levinsohn
Max Lowe
Michael "Mickey" Maher
Rachel Maillelle
Tim Manwaring
Ted Mattson
Sam Maxwell
Bill Mayer
Debbie McKinney
Chuck McMahan
Jules Mead
Susan Mellin
Shelley Metcalf
Phillip Meyer
Dave Mills
Catherine and Donald Mormile
Bruce Moroney
Tim Mowry
Carolyn Muegge-Vaughan
George Murphy
Stuart Nelson
Jack Niggemyer
Mark Nordman
Chris O'gar
Jim Okonek
Rich Owens
Chris Pamiptchuk
Ed Peck
Rosemary Phillips
Pascale Pibot

Larry and Brenda Plessinger
Pat Plunkett
Joanne Potts
Greg Probst
Leo Rasmussen
Joe Redington, Sr. and Vi Redington
Alan Reed
Pookie Reed
Bill Remmer
Libby Riddles
Harvey Rookus
Debbie Rork
Susan Ruddy
Peter and Tracy Schneiderheinze
Jeff Schultz
Del Seeba
Ralph Seekins
Bob Sept
Kent Sheets
Sirius Publishing
Judy Smith
Paul Souders
Barry Stanley
Harley Steward
Rick and Kathy Swenson
Dorothea Taylor
Mike Taylor
Lorraine Temple
John Thiede
Scott Thompson
Kristy Ticknor
Dick Tozier
John Tracy
Tony Turinski
Ken Ulz
Doug Van Reeth
Jim Varsos
Norman Vaughan
George Wagner
Denny Weber
Mark and Sheri Weinberger
Jeff Weintraub
Jim Welch
Jennifer Wolk
Yukon Quest Committee